136TH EDITION

# Thomas
# WINSDEN's
## CRICKETING ALMANACK

136TH EDITION

# Thomas
# WINSDEN's
## CRICKETING ALMANACK

# Vernon Coleman

CHILTON DESIGNS

Chilton Designs Publishers
Preston House, Kentisbury, Barnstaple, Devon EX31 4NH

First published in the United Kingdom by Severn House in
1983

British Library Cataloguing in Publication Data
Coleman, Vernon
    Thomas Winsden's cricketing almanack.
    1. Cricket—Anecdotes, faceial, satire, etc
    I. Title
    796.35'8'0207    GV919

    ISBN 1 8981 4600 2

Printed and bound in Great Britain by
The Bath Press, Avon

ILLUSTRATED BY DON ROBERTS

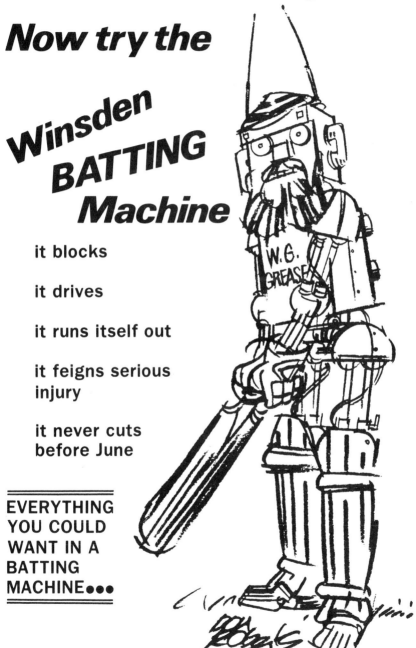

# FOR CRICKETOMEMORABILIA UNLIMITED . . .

## . . . VISIT CRICKETOMEMORABILIA UNLIMITED

For . . .
. . . the box worn by Victor Trumper's brother
. . . photographs of Yorkshire gatemen smiling
. . . two buttons from one of Fred Trueman's shirts
. . . and more!

For . . .
. . . sawdust used on the famous Headingley pitch
. . . an ice box confiscated during the Perth Test of the tour of 82/3
. . . chewing gum taken from the bat of Alexander Woolcott
. . . the ball used by Freddie Laker in his famous Test Match
. . . and much more!

For . . .
. . . a coke can clattered during the '79 Gillette Cup Final
. . . an A to Z map of Lahore
. . . a transistor radio on which the voice of John Arlott has been heard
. . . and much, much more!

---

Contact:
**Cricketomemorabilia Unlimited** – the biggest collection of cricketomemorabilia on ANY offshore island.

*CRICKETOMEMORABILIA, Lundy Island.*

# Winsden Electrically Heated Personal Protector

# TOXTETH's
# LITTLE NIPPLE GUARDS

*HYGIENIC!*

*SELF ADHESIVE!*

*AVAILABLE IN 16 DIFFERENT SIZES*

A **MUST** *for all women cricketers*

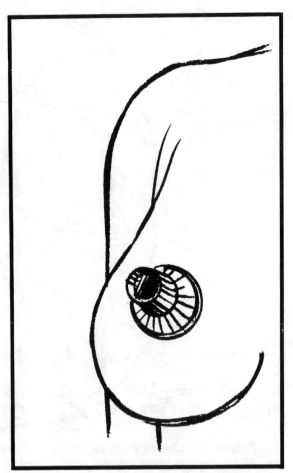

# Toxteth's of Liverpool
*Serving women for over one hundred years.*

# ★ COVER
## MIDDLE AND LEG · · ·
### and the other bits too!
★

**Digby Arrowsmith and Eve St. Lawrence are proud to announce that their current spring collection includes the first unisex cricket ensemble.**
The basic collection consists of:

☆ Shiny white patent leather pumps with a modest heel to give the shorter player a little extra height.

☆ Flared, white silk slacks with beaded edging and knitted waistband. Seat area made out of matching shrink-fit white denim.

☆ Silk shirt or blouse with pearl buttons and 'sailor-boy' collar, flared sleeves and puckered wrist bands.

☆ Crew-neck sleeveless cardigan, buttoned at the front in waistcoat style. Made from white mohair and embroidered with your team colours and insignia.

☆ Crew-neck sleeved cardigan buttoned at the front in jacket style. Made from white six-ply baby wool and embroidered with your team colours.

☆ Peakless French beret in the colours of your choice.

*In addition Digby Arrowsmith and Eve St. Lawrence are now sole agents for:*
*Gucci's over-the-shoulder silk-lined cricket bag*
*Playertex 'hug-as-you-run' chest protector (34A to 44DD)*
*"Cosi-kit" bespoke box makers — made to measure abdominal protectors (outsize a speciality)*

# MAKING SANDWICHES?

Bored with eggs, cheese, cress, ham and tomato?
Fed up with boring old lobster meat and caviare?
Sick of plovers' eggs?

Then why not try **WALL-PAPA PASTE?**

It's the sandwich spread with a difference you'll notice . . .
. . . a burgundy paste with more than a hint of sophistication
. . . the delicious tang of fresh oranges
. . . the mouth watering flavour of melons
. . . the excitement of fresh vodka in a 100% proof
. . . the deep sea taste of roll mop herring
. . . the bitter sweet poignancy of chocolate
. . . the arrogance of coconut
. . . the rich, friendly fire of English mustard
. . . the smooth, rich nourishment of porridge oats
All in traditional, original, exclusive WALL-PAPA PASTE

"It's something you'll never forget!" says Geoffrey Ballcock

# UMPIRES .... *You need*
# Winsden's Matched Pebble Set

*for easy, confident counting in all types of cricket. Each pebble is carefully picked by hand and polished by machine.*

(actual size)

**Look at what these leading umpires have to say about Winsden's Matched Pebbles**

"I count on them" – D. Bird

"A pleasure to handle" – D. Burd

"I wish these had been available when I started my career" – D. Byrd

"A major contribution to safer ball-counting" – D. Berd

# Foreword

When this book was first published, and review copies were sent out, I received several angry telephone calls from sports writers telling me that the printers had misspelt the title. I think it is, therefore, appropriate for me to introduce this new edition of Winsden with a short explanation.

Thomas Winsden was born in 1811 in the village of Headingley. In 1826 he moved with his parents to London where his father, a far seeing entrepreneur, bought a half share in a petrol station. When lack of custom forced the station's closure Winsden Senior died of shame leaving young Thomas in charge of the family which consisted of five sisters and five brothers as well as the grieving Winsden widow.

Fired by hunger and a sense of responsibility, Thomas unearthed a small printing set (received as a Christmas present some years earlier) and with this he set up a business in the kitchen of their modest home. After small successes as a jobbing printer he founded Thomas Winsden's Sporting Guidebooks and began with annuals for lovers of such sports as cock fighting and bear baiting. In 1847 Winsden responded to demand from cricket lovers throughout the country by preparing his first Cricketing Almanack.

Unfortunately this exciting new project never reached the bookstalls. A fire in the Winsden kitchen destroyed the letters F–N and a shortage of capital reserves meant that the budding publisher was unable to stay in business.

From 1847 until his death in 1896 Thomas Winsden wrote out longhand version of all his book—including the Cricketing Almanack—but sadly none of the manuscripts have survived. From 1897 to 1982 Winsden's descendants continued the tradition by writing and then carefully losing, yearly editions of the Almanack.

In 1982 the sole surviving member of the Winsden family died in a tragic stump-sharpening accident and I took over the responsibility for producing the Almanack. So, although this is, in fact, the 136th edition of the Almanack (making it the longest established Sporting Year Book in the world) it is the first volume to be available to the public.

I think Thomas would have been quite pleased with the first publicly available edition of this Almanack. Winsden was a great fan of overseas cricket and would have been pleased to see details of Australian Beach Cricket included together with the latest French Cup Rules and scores from the amazing Curry Cup held in India.

Winsden himself was a great statistician and our statistics section contains details of the frst Umpires' Averages Table together with a unique Sandwich Making Averages Table. (This shows that although cheese and tomato has been the dominant force at club level there is room for variety since Mrs Pettifer, the winner, was a specialist in egg and cress.)

Finally, I believe that it is usual on these occasions for the editor to include a line taking all responsibilities for errors and omissions. Well, bugger that. I would like to blame the sub editor, the printer, my secretary and everyone in the bar at the Duck and Puddle for the errors and omissions which undoubtedly mar the accuracy of this slim volume.

Vernon Coleman
Devon 1994

# CONTENTS

# Review of the year

## THE 1982 CURRY CUP
*(India's premier tournament)*

The Curry Cup has been an established part of the Indian cricket scene for seven years now. Since the trophy was first introduced by the Prime Minister's nephew it has proved popular with players and spectators alike.

Unhappily, the 1982 season will be remembered not for the quality of the cricket played, but for the way in which the organisers of the Curry Cup tried to cope with the problems caused by the dreadful weather which affected India for most of the season.

Normally the Indian cricket season is blessed with fine weather. In 1982, however, there were storms for so much of the season that the first matches in the Curry Cup could not be played until a month before the final was due to take place.

With the agreement of the various teams involved the organisers solved this problem by arranging for several matches to be played at once. It was decreed that not only should matches be played at the same time but on the same ground.

So it was that at precisely ten o'clock in the morning, one Friday in late summer, umpires R.S. Vasudevan, N.Y. Mathur, S. Bhanot, V. Parkar, D. Krishnan and S. Satham all strode onto the pitch to signal the start of play in the matches between Baroda and Bombay,

Uttar Pradesh and Delhi and Haryana and Tamnilnadu.

To begin with, everything went remarkably smoothly. Chapro and Minkad opened the bowling for Bombay, Geol and Ashok opened the bowling for Delhi and Jeeva and Kamar opened the bowling for Haryana. With all thirty three members of the three fielding sides on the pitch there weren't many opportunities for scoring in the first session and by lunch none of the sides had reached double figures.

After lunch there were one or two difficulties to be ironed out. The three umpires complained that they had difficulty in deciding which ball they were supposed to be watching and one of the batsmen complained that the other two wouldn't take their fair share of standing in front of the wicket and risking an LBW decision. Two of the three wicket keepers had a brawl which resulted in the loser being taken from the pitch with a broken clavicle.

By tea time, the Baroda team had all been dismissed and Bombay had come out to bat. Again there were problems because the three umpires couldn't decide whether or not the pitch should be rolled. Eventually they decided that a third of it should be rolled. Then there was the question of which third to choose. They were still arguing when one of the Delhi bowlers delivered a fast off-break and dismissed three batsmen all at once. They all contrived to touch the ball on its way to the three wicket keepers who then succeeding in catching it together.

By the second day, some of the batsmen were getting used to the problems of deciding which ball to hit, some of the bowlers were growing accustomed to tripping over slower bowlers on their way in to the wicket and some of the umpires were beginning to overcome the difficulty inherent in trying to decide which batsman had run out which batsman. But the fielders were still in a dreadful quandary. They kept chasing the wrong ball, running after the wrong ball and bumping into one another. Four silly points may be able to fit in alongside one another, but there really isn't room on a cricket square for nine short legs.

Things got worse on the third day when the administrators decided that because of the backlog they would have to start matches between Bombay and Delhi, Uttar Pradesh and Baroda and Railways and Airways before those in progress had finished. This meant that there were six separate matches being played on the same wicket and that several teams were playing in two matches at once.

Some of the commentators and reporters at the games complained that all this had made the 1982 Curry Cup laughable and had detracted from the value of the competition as a sporting spectacle.

While argument continued in the press box, there were fresh signs of trouble on the pitch. When a Bombay player complained that a Delhi player had handled one of their balls, a scorer took advantage of the lull to run on to the pitch and ask which side had just scored a boundary. None of the umpires knew anything about this and the confusion was made worse when an argument broke out about the ownership of the 17 cricket balls which were in use. One spectator ran on and claimed that two of the balls were his, while an umpire apologised and said that some of the balls had fallen out of his pocket by mistake.

While one of the umpires sent off one of the players for arguing, two batsmen struggled to retrieve a ball from the grasp of a small boy who claimed that he was playing in an Under 15 Colts team league match and an appeal from a Bombay player resulted in four umpires holding up their fingers at once.

With the sun setting over the pavilion, the umpires went into a huddle and interviewed all the captains separately. Ten minutes later it was announced that the newest side (and, incidentally, the richest) in the tournament, the Bengal Lions, had won the 1982 Curry Cup. The umpires then left quickly for holidays in the Caribbean.

# A GREAT MOMENT FOR ENGLISH SPECTATORS

When the England twelfth man dropped the drinks tray during the 89th match with Australia in last winter's Bunsen and Hodges tournament, captain Bob Willis announced that he was so fed up with the team's unprofessional attitude that he was prepared to give a few amateurs a game.

As a result, there were lots of new faces in the 90th match. Opening the batting for England were Mr and Mrs Hubert Pilsbury from Swindon. The Pilsburys had flown to Australia to visit their married daughter and had visited the Melbourne Cricket Ground by mistake, thinking it was the local maternity hospital. They were both surprised (though delighted) to find themselves opening batpeople.

Batting at number three was octagenarian Gilbert Padlock who told reporters that he had watched one-day cricket several times and had played table cricket with his grandson on several occasions. Because of his tactical experience he was made vice-captain.

Wilhelm Spassky was at number four. He told me that he never thought he'd get a chance to play cricket for England after he lost his legs in a mining accident. He insisted that his bilateral cataracts were of no real significance.

At numbers five and six were the eight-year-old Hoover twins who had gone to Australia with their mother. She was batting at number seven and was also down on the card as wicket keeper.

The player at number eight, Dick Barton, a retired private investigator, was in the team as a fast bowler rather than a batsman. He assured Willis that he had once played rounders with his sister.

Alexander Haig, at 93 the oldest player in the side, knew that he would have to carry a pair of crutches as well as his bat when he took to the field but he seemed confident as he replaced his truss with a personal protector. He was down to bat at number nine.

With 'Blind' Willy Festhinger, the jazz pianist, at ten and Willis himself at eleven the team had a convincing look to it. Nonetheless, most Australians were surprised when the English team won by nine wickets. Aussie captain Kim Hughes said she thought it was a pity the new team hadn't been given an airing sooner. She told startled pressmen that she thought England would have made the final had they played the same team in earlier matches.

### *Footnote*
The England touring party sat in the spectators' enclosure for this match. They did not do well. Three injured themselves while clapping, two fell over while fetching beer, one was ejected from the ground for insulting behaviour, four dropped litter and were arrested and the rest all got lost in the toilets.

### Bunsen and Hodges Cup – 1985
The 1985 Bunsen and Hodges Cup will again involve Australia, New Zealand and England. This time, however, there will be more matches. To begin with, each team will play the other two teams 78 times. Then the top three teams will play each other again. This round will consist of 56 matches. When those matches have been played the top three teams will play a knock-out competition consisting of 489 matches. The top three teams will then play in a prolonged final which will last

for three and a half years. At the end of that time the top three teams will each receive huge cheques, a trophy, a bag full of medals and an invitation to take part in the next Bunsen and Hodges Cup.

---

**Over Rates 1983**
The National Union of Bowlers (NUB) has negotiated new rates for professional bowlers working for league clubs on a piece-work basis. In future bowlers will be paid 75p per over bowled with a 25p bonus for each maiden.

---

# THE 1982 SINGLE WICKET COMPETITION

Last year, for the first time ever, club cricketers were invited to take part in a national single wicket competition. Nearly six hundred individual clubs entered for the contest which was sponsored by a company which asked to be allowed to remain anonymous. In view of the success of the competition the company's decision was probably a wise one.

In theory the competition should have proved attractive; unfortunately the sponsors insisted on allowing their own copywriter to prepare the official list of rules.

Not being familiar with cricket, the copy-writer, a middle-aged lady of Austrian extraction more accustomed to writing ads that enticed housewives to purchase extra quantities of soap powder, misunderstood the basic concept and applied the rules so that they would fit a literal translation of the competition's title.

Batsmen found the regulations extremely appealing, but bowlers did not enjoy the competition at all. Although a total of 754 matches were played during the months of the competition only two batsmen were given out 'bowled', none were given out lbw and only three were 'run out'. No batsmen were given out 'hit wicket' and no batsmen were given out 'stumped'. The remainder of the 73 wickets which fell during the competition went to catches.

With the rules favouring batsmen so heavily there were, naturally, some high scores. Lord Thackelay's XI, for example, scored 945 for two wickets in one of their early matches. The Leamington Cricket Club managed 879 for one in a second round match and the Lydeard St. Lawrence team lost only three wickets while piling up a total of 987.

Because of the difficulty of getting batsmen out, the competition lasted for much longer than had been expected. The match between Lord Thackelay's XI and the Hampstead 2nd XI went on for seven and half days and nights; a match between Newbury and Wichampton went on for 147 hours without a break; and a game played between Glasgow Celtic and Little Hampton took up 17 Sundays.

In the end the competition was won by those with the stamina to keep going. Lord Thackelay's XI, overjoyed at the prospect of winning a match for the first time in the club's history, were the only team willing to attend the final at Lords in late October. They won by default.

There will be no official single wicket competition in 1983.

---

**Women at Lords**
Suitably dressed women will, in future, be allowed to buy chocolates and sweets from the small shop at Lords as long as they have in their possession written permission from a member. Women will still not be allowed to buy cigarettes, tobacco or matches, however.

---

# FRENCH CRICKET CHAMPIONSHIPS: 1982

For the third year running, the French cricket championship challenge cup was won by the widely respected Dijon team which has now accumulated a record of major championship wins matched only by the legendary Calais Cricketers XI, which so dominated French cricket in the 1930s.

One of the disadvantages and difficulties of French cricket (so far as classically trained cricketers are concerned) is the fact that knee and ankle movements are essential to success.

René Renault, the Dijon team captain and coach, has made no secret of the fact that these days he prefers to recruit fresh squad members from the ballet companies of Paris, London and Moscow rather than from the cricket teams of England, Australia or South Africa. 'Ballet dancers,' he argues with convincing logic, 'have the fluidity of movement which enables them to defend through the full three hundred and sixty degree range.'

He points to Alphonse de Peugeot and Ricardo Gauloise, both regular members of this year's successful squad, as evidence that his training and selection philosophy is a sound one. De Peugeot was, of course, an Assistant Senior Principal dancer with the youth section of the Melbourne Festival Ballet Company but since he failed to grow more than an inch or two above five feet his career came to a halt. He just didn't have the height or strength to pick up any of the ballerinas.

Fortunately for de Peugeot, the Master of the Corps de Ballet in Melbourne, Dustin Le Coin, had for many years enjoyed a close personal relationship with René Renault. Advice in the young dancer's ear took him straight to Dijon where, after an introductory trial game, de Peugeot was offered a three year contract.

For Gauloise the route to success was not dissimilar.

After several years with the Durban Ballet Company, Gauloise (his father was an international sales executive with a major French oil company) became allergic to nylon. Unable to wear tights of any description, but unable to dance without them, he was forced to seek some other outlet for his talents.

With players like de Peugeot and Gauloise in his team, Renault is confident about the future. He believes that the Dijon squad can continue to dominate French cricket. The evidence suggests that his confidence is not misplaced.

### Changes in the rules of French cricket for the 1983 season

The International Board of French cricket control and the Marie-le-os Cricket Club have, after consultation, significantly changed the rules for French cricket. As a service to readers of the *Thomas Winsden's Cricketing Almanack* we are reproducing the new rules here in their entirety.

1. If the match is an official IBFCC meeting, then each team shall consist of one captain and ten players.

2. If the match is an informal, impromptu one then the two captains shall appoint themselves and then select teams by picking from the then available players. The captains shall choose alternately and if there is an odd number of players then the captain choosing second shall have the extra player.

3. The two captains shall toss a coin to decide who bats first. The coin shall be allowed to land on the ground. It shall be returned to its rightful owner after the 'toss' has been read.

4. The batsman shall stand with his feet together and facing due North. (Or in the opposite direction to any greenhouse, pair of French windows or other large expanse of glass). He shall be equipped with a cricket bat which shall be no more than twenty four inches long

and four inches wide.

5. The bowler shall stand ten feet away and shall be equipped with a soft ball no more than six inches in diameter.

6. The fielders shall stand around. They shall stand at least three feet away from the batsman.

7. After shouting 'ready' the bowler shall throw, roll, toss or bowl the ball towards the batsman's legs using top spin, back spin, side spin or no spin as he sees fit. If the ball hits the batsman's legs on or below the knees, then the batsman shall be given out. The batsman shall also be given out if any fielder catches the ball directly off the bat or if a fielder catches the ball with one hand when it has bounced no more than once. If there is disagreement about whether or not the batsman is out then the fielders shall be invited to make a democratic decision as a sub-committee. If the ball is lost then the batsman is certainly out and there will be no argument about this.

8. After hitting the ball the batsman shall not move but shall be awarded runs by the fielding side according to the distance the ball has travelled.

9. The fielder who collects the ball shall automatically become the bowler and shall bowl from the position where the ball stopped. The bowler shall become a fielder. The batsman shall continue to stand with his feet together and facing due North. The rules for dismissal shall remain the same.

10. Anyone who does not play the game fairly shall be smacked and sent to bed without any.

+++

**Apology**

We apologise for the fact that, due to unforseeable circumstances, the answers to last year's quiz do not appear in this edition of *Thomas Winsden's Cricketing Almanack.*

They will probably be included in next year's edition

of the *Almanack*, if we can remember the questions. This year's *Almanack* contains no quiz.

# THE WORLD BEACH CRICKET CHAMPIONSHIPS 1982

For the eighth consecutive year the World Beach Championships were held on Bondi Beach, Australia and again won by the Sydney Heralds who beat their old rivals the Deauville Buccaneers by nine runs.

Since new rules had been revised stipulating that the driftwood used for the wickets must be no smaller than three foot tall and eight inches wide and no larger than four foot tall and twelve inches wide, batsmen had a much harder job defending their positions. The new bat regulations helped, of course. Until a year ago beach cricket batsmen had to use standard sized tennis rackets; this year, for the first time, batsmen were allowed to use beach tennis bats of almost any size.

Ace Sydney Herald bowler Steven Frieberg, who can turn an old tennis ball square on semi-dry sand, mesmerised the Deauville batsmen until a short, sharp shower took the bite out of the pitch and gave seamer Neville Chamberlaid more help.

Between the two of them Frieberg and Chamberlaid took all ten Deauville wickets and left the Buccaneers defending a total of a mere 146. Frieberg finished with six for thirty eight while Chamberlaid ended up with a career best of 4 for 46.

Sydney started their innings just as a gentle breeze off the sea started to waft fresh sand across the pitch. As a result, the ball bounced no more than a foot off the ground, so the Sydney openers had difficulty for the first few overs and it looked as though Deauville might do the impossible after all.

Then, much to the relief of the Sydney Heralds, the

breeze stopped and the drying sun quickly baked the top layer of sand, with the result that batsmen Harvey Wallbanger and Cliff Michaels could pat down a few square feet of level grains. With the ball rising predictably and gathering an even bounce from the pitch, the game quickly drifted in Sydney's favour. By tea they were 87 for no wicket and despite a courageous burst of seam bowling by Deauville ace Francois Mitterand the Heralds won the match fairly comfortably, reaching 147 with the loss of only three wickets.

After their victory the Sydney Heralds celebrated with ice creams and a dip in the sea.

---

**Fielding Circles**
It is now widely accepted in fielding circles, that when two players work as a sub-team unit to field a ball then the player who returns the ball to the wicket-keeper should be the one to acknowledge the applause of the crowd. The other player should do no more than blush modestly.

---

# THE BERT PLAYER LEAGUE
*Unexpected Win for Cumberland Tigers*

After several undistinguished seasons, Cumberland Tigers finally managed to end their lean patch with a spectacular win in the Bert Player League. Their success this year can be attributed to several factors.

First and foremost, of course, has been their marvellous Youth Cricket policy as a result of which hundreds of young people throughout the area have been encouraged to enjoy the pleasures of bowling and batting in organised coaching conditions. The Summer and Winter Cricket Schools, run by the side's Youth Training Manager, have likewise attracted many youngsters.

The money raised by many specially organised raffles, dances and sweepstakes has been used to build an indoor cricket school, complete with artificial wickets, netting over the windows and clever little metal cages over the light bulbs. The indoor school has made it possible for the first team to practice even in deepest winter and there is no doubt in the mind of the team coach that this facility has contributed to the team's spectacular success.

Groundsman Harry Patches has made his mark, too. His pitches have been true and well-prepared – and nothing gives batsmen more confidence than the knowledge that the concrete on which they are playing has been thoroughly swept and specially cleaned for the match in progress. A stray pebble or half-brick can ruin a batsman's style.

The new team manager, Brynmor Davis and the club secretary Davis Brynmor have succeeded in sharing all the administrative chores; this has enabled captain Vladek Jones to concentrate all his energies on making sure that his team has been 'psyched-up'. Ably assisted by his vice captain Majid Ganter, Jones has succeeded in moulding an effective and happy side. With no fewer than nine players who have passed through the colts' team and the second eleven in the side, the Cumberland Tigers are to be congratulated on their well deserved success.

Their two overseas players, Zahir Flaymore and Nick Walters, who joined the side this year for the first time, will be staying with the Cumberland Tigers for the coming season although both will have to miss some matches because of Test calls.

## Cumberland Tigers
*Averages*

### Batting Averages

| Name | Place of birth | Matches | Innings | Not out | Runs | Average |
|------|---------------|---------|---------|---------|------|---------|
| Z. Flaymore | Melbourne | 22 | 34 | 7 | 2557 | 94.7 |
| N. Walters | Karachi | 22 | 34 | 5 | 2532 | 87.3 |
| M. Ganter | Cumberland | 22 | 33 | 3 | 186 | 6.4 |
| V. Jones | Cumberland | 22 | 28 | 5 | 74 | 3.2 |
| V. Brown | Cumberland | 22 | 31 | 11 | 62 | 3.1 |
| K. Carter | Cumberland | 22 | 29 | 2 | 78 | 2.9 |
| L. Smith | Cumberland | 22 | 17 | 9 | 18 | 2.3 |
| O. Peters | Cumberland | 22 | 18 | 4 | 25 | 1.8 |
| R. Ford | Cumberland | 22 | 22 | 3 | 23 | 1.19 |
| S. Russell | Cumberland | 22 | 26 | 8 | 18 | 1.02 |
| W. Simpson | Cumberland | 22 | 25 | 4 | 6 | 0.3 |

### Bowling Averages

| Name | Place of birth | Overs | Maidens | Runs | Wickets | Average |
|------|---------------|-------|---------|------|---------|---------|
| N. Walters | Karachi | 567 | 438 | 154 | 123 | 1.25 |
| Z. Flaymore | Melbourne | 593 | 421 | 169 | 108 | 1.56 |
| V. Jones | Cumberland | 76 | 3 | 538 | 11 | 48.9 |
| S. Russell | Cumberland | 45 | 1 | 673 | 8 | 84 |
| R. Ford | Cumberland | 23 | 0 | 5,444 | 2 | 2722 |

### Fielding

### Catches

Walters (72 caught)    Flaymore (66 caught)    Ford, Russell, Peters (1 caught each)

---

**Young Tourists**
The Nannycare Under Nines England Tourists opened their tour of New Zealand with a resounding win over an Auckland Representative Schools Side.

Unfortunately, eight members of the touring party who were suffering from acute homesickness had to return home immediately after the match and the remaining fixtures were subsequently cancelled.

---

# ORGANISING CRICKET
*A brief look at the activities of the various governing bodies during the last twelve months*

### January
The Advisory County Cricket Committee met at Lords and decided to call a special meeting of the World Cricket Conference in June. The National Cricket Association's treasury sub-committee sent a memorandum to the Association of Cricket Control asking that the Board of Cricket Supervision examine the question of changing the lbw law. The Cricket Council and the Marylebone Cricket Club met to decide whether or not to reorganise the Test and Country Cricket Board. The International Cricket Board's disciplinary sub-committee met to discuss the Council of Cricket Bodies. The Board of Cricket called for a meeting of the Cricket Association.

### February
The Cricket Council and the Board of Cricket Supervision sent a report to the International Cricket Board asking them to reconsider last year's decision to start one-day games at 8.0am. The Council of Cricket Bodies sent a deputation to the Cricket Association. The Cricketing Control Supervising Council sent a deputation to the Council of Cricket Bodies.

### March
The Council of Cricket Bodies sent a deputation to the Cricketing Control Supervising Council. The Cricket Association sent a deputation to the Council of Cricket Bodies. The Marylebone Cricket Club decided to hold a meeting.

### April
The World Cricket Association's Players' Committee

met with the International Cricket Association's Players' Committee and decided to appoint a delegate to the Cross-Continental Cricket Association's Players' Committee. The Cross-Continental Cricket Association's Players' Committee and the International Cricket Association's Players' Committee met and decided to appoint a delegate to the World Cricket Association's Players' Committee. The World Cricket Association's Players' Committee and the Cross-Continental Cricket Association's Players' Committee met and decided to appoint a delegate to the International Cricket Association's Players' Committee.

## May
The World Cricket Association's Players' Committee, the International Cricket Association's Players' Committee and the Cross-Continental Cricket Association's Players' Committee were all amalgamated into the World, International and Cross-Continental Cricket Associations' Players' Committee.

## June
The World Cricket Conference met and decided to call a meeting of the Advisory County Cricket Committee in January.

## July
The Council of Cricket Bodies and the Board of Cricket formed a joint committee to discuss the question of whether or not the International Cricket Board should be disbanded.

## August
The International Cricket Board and the Council of Cricket Bodies decided that the Board of Cricket should be disbanded. The Test and Country Cricket Board met to discuss the lbw law. The National Cricket

Association's printing sub-committee met.

### September
The Board of Cricket Supervision and the International Cricket Board sent a report to the Cricket Council asking them to reconsider the decision to start one day games at 7.0 am.

### October
The Cricket Council and the Test and Country Cricket Board met to discuss the possibility of forming a sub-committee to discuss the question of whether or not the Advisory County Cricket Committee should have a sub-committee to discuss the National Cricket Association's ability to form fresh committees.

### November
The Council of Cricket Bodies met to discuss the disciplinary committee of the International Cricket Board.

### December
The Cricket Council sent a card to the Board of Cricket Supervision and the Council of Cricket Bodies sent a card to the Cricketing Control Supervising Council. The Council of Cricket Bodies sent a card to the Cricketing Control Committee and the Marylebone Cricket Club sent cards to everyone.

+++

### Finance and the counties
Figures released by the Test and Country Cricket Board show that the seventeen first class counties gained income from the following sources during the last twelve month period:

|                  |            |
|------------------|------------|
| Sponsorship:     | £8,947,397 |
| Advertising:     | £6,398,290 |
| Television fees: | £5,439,201 |

31

Bar receipts:     £243,926,849
Admission fees:   £14.90
Scorecard sales:  £0.82

# AROUND THE COUNTIES
*An annual look at the individual cricketing counties*

### Derbyshire
Once again there have been contractual problems at Derbyshire. Four players were offered two year contracts and two players were offered four year contracts while three players were offered one year contracts and one player was offered a three year contract. Three of the four players who were offered two year contracts accepted and one of the three players who were offered one year contracts accepted. The player who was offered a three year contract declined but both players who were offered four year contracts accepted. The man who writes the clubs contracts was offered a five year contract.

### Essex
Few sides are as happy as Essex. With several confirmed practical jokers in the team, a laugh is never far away. Gales of hysterical mirth marked the team's disappearance from the Banker's Trophy and when they lost a vital County Championship match early in the season, some of the players ended up laughing so much that they had to be carried off the field. One or two members of the side can always be counted on to put superglue on the spot where the bowler starts his run-up, or to encourage the entire team to wear sixteen sweaters each on a hot day so that the umpires risk heat-prostration. Doubtless, Essex will continue to give great pleasure to us all for many seasons to come.

## Glamorgan

The only Welsh county team had a tremendous season. Jones and Jones opened the bowling with fire and vigour and were well supported by the two medium pacers Jones and Jones. One of the established opening batsmen, Jones, lost his place to newcomer Jones in May and halfway through the season the other established opener, Jones, lost his place to a second newcomer called Jones. The leading scorer was again the indomitable Jones and the captain and vice-captain, Jones and Jones respectively were reappointed. Wicket-keeper Jones retired at the end of the summer but reserve keeper Slougupta is expected to do well in the forthcoming season.

## Gloucestershire

With cash availability a real problem in Bristol, Gloucestershire are being forced to cut costs. In future players will travel to away matches by bicycle. Attempts will be made to ensure that no innings played by the home side needs more than one new ball and the scoreboard will only be operated when someone is actually looking at it.

## Hampshire

Members of the Hampshire club are beginning to think that the Test selectors have forgotten their team exists. After winning the four major trophies for the last six successive seasons, Hampshire must have thought that some of their players would have been entitled to expect international recognition. Not a bit of it! Even the county's star all rounder failed to get an England cap – despite scoring 3,496 runs in the season at an average of 103, taking 149 wickets at an average of 11 and holding 64 catches. Still, perhaps another good season will do the trick.

## Kent

Kent's policy of giving young players a chance in the first team has produced several problems. Finding baby sitters during away matches has been particularly difficult. In addition there has been the problem of providing school lessons for some members of the team. Some embarrassment has resulted from the fact that the players have had to be provided with milk during the drinks intervals. Two players not yet weaned have required special services.

## Lancashire

Benefits, testimonials and appeals have been so successful in Lancashire that it has been decided to concentrate all the county's future efforts on fund raising. The county will sell raffle and sweepstake tickets rather than scorecoards and instead of a fixture list members will be given a diary of special fund raising events. Shares in the county team are to be quoted on the stock market within the next two years.

## Leicestershire

In an exciting managerial move, the Leicestershire Commercial Management Team have announced that forthcoming first-class county matches will be designed to start at whatever time is deemed most suitable by the spectators. Both regular spectators will be telephoned at 9.0 am every match day and asked to nominate a time. The mean of their two recommendations will be taken as the official start-time. Play will end when the two spectators have to go home.

## Middlesex

Problems with the balance of the side meant that F. Titmole had to be recalled to the team yet again. Because of his advancing years, Titmole was given permission by the T.C.C.B. to approach the wicket in a wheelchair but several umpires complained about the tracks being made on the pitch and Titmole had to approach the wicket under his own steam for the remainder of the season. Titmole's success, however, encouraged the Middlesex selectors to recall other former players and by the end of the season Crompton, Hendon, Edwich, Man, Murry, Parfait and Hearn had joined Titmole, Allan, Robbins and Pebbles.

## Northampton

The Northampton side has been so successful despite its weak bowling line-up that the county's selection committee has decided to do away with bowlers altogether. In the coming seasons the committee will select eleven batsmen and leave the captain to sort out the bowling problems as best as he can. One suggested batting line-up for Northampton looks as though it could easily be reversed without attracting any comment. It will be interesting to see how successful the experiment is.

## Nottinghamshire

Injury problems at Trent Bridge have meant more problems for the selectors. When the New Zealand fast bowler was fit the South African all rounder was injured but when the Pakistani fast bowler was injured the Indian all rounder was fit. The South African all rounder's injury got better at about the same time as the Indian all rounder sustained an injury and the New Zealand faster bowler went on the sick list at the same time as the Pakistani fast bowler became fit enough to rejoin the team.

## Somerset

Few counties can claim to have spectators as enthusiastic and as partisan as those who follow the fortunes of Somerset. For that reason, it's unsurprising that when

Somerset's newly formed Followers' Club decided to raise a little extra money by putting some of its members on the transfer list, many eager offers should be made. After lengthy negotiations, four spectators were finally transferred to Gloucestershire and four to Lancashire. Nottinghamshire and Leicestershire are currently reported to be negotiating for additional fans in the hope that they, too, will be able to benefit from fresh vocal support.

## Surrey

Once they were the most successful and famous side in the land. These days, however, the Surrey cricket team is no longer a force to be reckoned with. As a pointer to their reduced stature in the modern world of professional cricket it is perhaps worth mentioning that when the fixture list for the current season was originally prepared, Surrey was completely left out of the reckoning. The names of the other sixteen county sides were fed into the computer but the name of Surrey was left out. The result of this unhappy oversight was that the Surrey manager found himself ringing round the other counties and pub sides, looking for a few games to keep his players occupied. Happily the latest news is that he has managed to arrange a considerable number of fixtures. To cover their confusion and embarrassment, the T.C.C.B. has agreed to regard all Surrey's friendly fixtures as first-class matches and to include the county in the reckoning for the County Championship. But it was a close shave. And quite a change from the days of Freddie Laker and the Bisto Twins.

## Sussex

They've found the secret of a balanced attack at Sussex. Aware that some counties suffer when they lose star Test players to touring sides, the Sussex committee has succeeded in putting together a perfect fast bowling combination! With a Pakistani and a South African leading the seam attack there is little risk of Sussex ever losing *both* players to a touring party.

### Warwickshire
The midland side had another tremendous season. The supporters club raised £193 billion with a scrip issue bull and stag amendment quotation of nearly £64 billion. This exceeded last year's total by £17 billion and enabled the side to buy a controlling interest in Esso, Westinghouse and General Motors. The club lent a total of £11 billion to other counties, built four new stands and purchased a huge plastic dome to cover the car park in the event of rain. The team came bottom in every competition for the eleventh successive year.

### Worcestershire
Heavy rain throughout the season meant that there were unusual problems at New Road. The river burst its banks in early April and didn't recede until the end of the season; this resulted in most of Worcestershire's matches being played under several inches of water. The problem was at its worst in July when the whole of the pitch was three feet beneath the surface level of the water. A Kent player who was bitten by a pike while fielding at short leg is apparently taking legal action against the club. The practise nets were, as usual, perfect.

### Yorkshire
A few minor personality clashes meant that the captaincy changed hands several times in Yorkshire. By May, every member of the playing staff had had a hand at leading the side, so the committee decided to introduce some fresh blood. For the month of June the captaincy was given to one of the scorecard sellers. In July it was entrusted to the Deputy Assistant Head Groundsman's Secretary. Disappointingly, however,

these imaginative changes produced less than impressive results, so in August Lord Hawke was disinterred and given the job for the remainder of the season.

The Yorkshire committee itself had to face some problems too. Traditionally, meetings have been held at Harrogate and Bradford as well as at Leeds but at the end of last season it was decided that no more meetings would be held at Harrogate because of the lack of suitable facilities adjoining the committee room there. This decision caused quite an uproar among the members of the committee – particularly those living in Harrogate. As a result of the confusion caused by this uproar a proposal to hold fewer meetings but to make them last for four days instead of three days had to be shelved.

# ADVANCES IN TECHNOLOGY
## *A Winsden Special Review*

At one time all you needed to play cricket was a bat, a ball and a handful of stumps. Over the years, though, cricket has become a far more complicated game. In an attempt to keep readers of *Thomas Winsden's Cricketing Almanack* up to date we have compiled a short directory to some of the seasons more startling innovations.

### The Magic Moisture Meter
You may have seen a simple, primitive version of this instrument in use on television. Today's new Magic Moisture Meter is a piece of technological wizardry. All the user has to do is insert a series of one hundred and twenty one-inch diameter probes into the pitch on a good length. The probes will then automatically measure the amount of water in the soil and give an instant reading on the Hi-Tech Joule Dial. This device is a must for all cricket captains, groundsmen, commenta-

tors and TV personalities who feel a burning need to look as though they know what they are talking about.

## The Whimple Grass Acceleration Rate Assessment Tool

Consisting of two simple, photoelectric cells powered by solar energy, the Whimple measures the rate at which grass grows. This sort of information is vital in helping the captain decide just how much grass is likely to be present on the pitch by the end of the day.

### Player's Comfort-Aid

If you've ever been concerned about just how much fluid cricketers lose on a hot day and how much they need to drink in order to replace it, then you'll be pleased to hear about the Player's Comfort-Aid. Designed by a former cricketer who once suffered a dry mouth for thirty-five minutes after an unprecedented fluid loss, the Players' Comfort-Aid measures skin galvanometry, atmospheric humidity and barometric incidence. A print-out facility ensures that the cricketer or his hydrotherapist can tell at once how low his fluid reserves are getting – and precisely when they'll need topping up. With the Player's Comfort-Aid station drinks intervals need never be arbitrary again.

### Ball Speed Assessor

This simple pocket device is just the thing for fielders. Before a match you programme in your peak acceleration rate and constant running speed. Then, when playing, you simply point the Assessor's radar beam at the ball as it leaves the bat. You must hold the ball in focus for a full two seconds.

Within an instant, the Ball Speed Assessor will tell you whether you can catch the ball or whether you might just as well let it go to the boundary where it will be fielded by a small boy.

## The Batsman's Friend

Although still in the experimental stages this device could revolutionize cricket. A small computer-controlled 'magic eye' is fitted into the batsman's helmet and designed to follow the ball as it leaves the bowler's hand. The magic eye measures pace, spin and swing as well as instantly estimating the flight, direction and pitch-point of the ball. Next, a micro-transmitter, also in the helmet, sends an appropriate signal to a receiver situated in the base of the bat handle. A minute, nuclear powered motor ensures that the appropriate response is made. All the batsman has to do is wear the helmet and hold the bat. One coach has already pointed out that this may be asking too much of today's batsmen and an attempt is being made to reduce the batsman's involvement still further.

## Umpire's Instant Aid

Television viewers have for some time had a chance to watch 'instant replays' when close decisions have to be made by umpires. Now, thanks to Olive St Clair, umpires will be able to watch these replays too.

A miniature television camera together with an equally small receiver ensures that the the umpire can get the benefit of an instant replay even when no television company is covering the match. With the Umpire's Instant Aid, controversy should soon be a thing of the past. Unfortunately, its introduction has been delayed by controversy.

## The Cricketer's Miniature Calculator

One-day cricket has made scoring infinitely more complicated. A match can often hinge on whether or not one side bowls the most overs, concedes the least runs or drinks the greatest quantity of lemon squash during the tea interval. This specially designed calculator is intended to help both batsmen and fielders decide on the best form of action to take. If you've ever wondered whether you should simply try to block the last ball or attempt to hit it out of the ground then this is the device for you. The Cricketer's Miniature Calculator can easily be fixed to the side of a bat handle or concealed in the peak of a cap.

### The Cricket Bat Strength Gauge

Have you ever wondered whether your bat can take much more punishment? Have you ever asked yourself whether it will crack at a critical moment? Well, it's now possible to answer such questions with the aid of the Cricket Bat Strength Gauge. All you do is saw your favourite bat into eight separate pieces and feed them – one by one – into the gauge. The meter reading will then tell you just how strong your bat was and just how long it would have lasted.

---

### Cricketers Swap Shirts

Cricketers seem to be picking up bad habits from footballers. At the end of a Lancashire League match last season the players in the two sides exchanged shirts as they left the field. A spokesperson for the Women's Cricket Association said she thought it unlikely that women cricketers would pick up the habit, although she did admit that one team had been approached by Playertex who suggested that they might be prepared to sponsor such an activity.

---

# THE FIRST TEST AT PERTH
*A special match report from our war reporter*
*E. Hemingway*

Right from the beginning this looked like being a rather special match. A trivial argument with the taxi driver who had taken me to the ground, and who then demanded the price of a new cab for his efforts, attracted the unwelcome attentions of a boistrous group of Eski-haulers who decided to offer a considerable amount of inconsequential advice to both the driver and myself. Within minutes, a previously peaceful discussion had become heated and angry. As a result the police and local ambulance service were soon busily loading would-be spectators into police vans and ambulances. A total of fourteen were wounded seriously enough to need hospital attention. An additional twenty-seven were arrested.

The arrival of the two captains on the field for the toss was the signal for a fresh outbreak of hostilities. A group of hod-carriers at third man discovered a specta-tor in their midst reading a copy of the *Guardian* and sensibly decided to hurl empty beer cans at his head until he agreed to behave more reasonably. Unfor-tunately, one of the cans missed the Englishman's head and landed in the middle of a crowd of clam-pickers from Tasmania. Ten minutes later the two teams were on the field, but twenty-three hod-carriers and clam-pickers were in hospital while a further forty-seven were helping the police with their enquiries.

As England began their innings, the spectators settled down to a good day's drinking. For the best part of ten minutes, you could hear nothing but the snap, crackle and pop of ring-pulls being separated from beer cans – a sound only occasionally punctuated by the thud of willow on leather as one or another of the Englishmen accidentally hammered boot with bat.

The calm was destroyed when an ambitious clod in the outer tried to ream both his nostrils at once. A beer-heavy dingo passing by was deeply insulted by the gesture and seconds later the police were playing xylo-phone music on half a hundred wooden tops. The final result was thirty-three more in hospital and fifty-nine extra prison cells filled.

Nothing much happened after that until the lunch interval, a time when Australian spectators traditionally throw quantities of food into the lake of beer filling their stomachs. Given that the average spectator's muscular co-ordination will have been adversely affected by alcoholic imbibition the task of successfully transferring a chicken leg from cooler to stomach often presents almost insurmountable problems.

In the event it was not a chicken leg that caused the next dramatic interlude in the days proceedings, but a cheese roll which escaped from its owner's grasp, rolled down a grassy bank and knocked over a half-full can of Fosters. Now, there are few things likely to enrage an Australian more than knocking over his Fosters when the first froth of the can is still fresh on his lip. The incident resulted in another sixty-eight spectators being taken from the ground and provided with alternative accommodation either at the local hospital or the nearest police station.

So far, none of the fighting had taken place without some sort of a reason. After lunch, however, the majority of those at the match had had so much to drink that almost anything was likely to trigger off an angry response. It seems possible, for example, that the brawl which started in the Press Tent, spread into the committee rooms, caused chaos in the pavilion and eventually engulfed the ground, began entirely as a result of a harmless misunderstanding.

Whatever the truth may be about the evolution of the incident, the fighting spread around the ground like herpes on a private beach. To begin with missiles consisted of nothing more dangerous than empty beer cans, chicken bones and plastic cutlery. Within five or ten minutes, however, the air was heavy with full 440 ml. beer cans, travelling at between 80 and 90 mph and traversing the entire breadth of the ground! Peaceful spectators, sitting in quiet corners, soon found themselves under fire from people they couldn't even see.

It is difficult to estimate just how many cans were in the air at any one time but I myself saw one enthusiast hurling cans at the rate of fifteen a minute and a colleague claims that he witnessed a record-breaking rate of twenty-two per minute.

By this time, of course, the players were lying down on the pitch to reduce the risk of being hit by a hail of aluminium. Attempts by one or two players to leave the field failed; in fact, one Australian was felled and seriously injured as he made for the safety of the team's underground dugout.

At the end of the day, when the police scorers added up their totals it seemed that a total of nine hundred and thirty-two spectators had been arrested and a hundred and ninety-three had been taken to hospital. These figures meant that the police, with none arrested and only a hundred and thirty-two taken to hospital, were comfortable winners.

### Editor's note

Our fearless war reporter was killed in the fighting which took place on the second day of the Test Match at Perth. As a veteran of riots and disruptions in India, Pakistan, Barbados and Taunton, Eddie Hemingway knew very well what risks he was taking by writing about cricket. He chose to do so, however, in the knowledge that his courage and skill gave solace to millions of faithful readers. We send our condolences to his families in Durban, Melbourne, Manchester, Karachi and Jamaica.

# WOMEN'S CRICKET COMES OF AGE

When the Shropshire Lasses XI (sponsored by Nusmear Petroleum Jelly) was invited to take part in the 1982

Angipax Drugs One Day Trophy Competition, history was made. Although women have been playing cricket for many decades, this was the first time that a women-only team had been invited to play in a competition which also involved the other first class teams.

To celebrate this important occasion we have decided to include pen portraits of the eleven members of the Shropshire Lasses XI (sponsored by Nusmear Petroleum Jelly) in this edition of the Almanack.

## Shropshire Lasses XI (Sponsored by Nusmear Petroleum Jelly)

### 1. Alice von Daniken (capt)
Alice learned her cricket with the help of her four older brothers. As a result of this early training she is an excellent out fielder. Hampered in her throwing by an over-developed chest, which she does her best to disguise with a Playertex Extra Strength Protector, Alice leads her players from the front. Although her bowling is perhaps best described as variable Alice often confuses opposition batspersons with her slow medium long hops.

### 2. Heather Hamilton (vice capt)
Included in the side as an opening batsperson, Heather has based her style on players such as 'Slasher' McKay, Terry Braille and Christine Travery. Aware of her responsibilities to her side, however, she has tried to treat the game rather more seriously than those three individuals. Together with the now deceased Jacqui Kenneally, Heather once enjoyed an opening partnership which resulted in her side declaring after three days with a score of 37 for no wickets.

### 3. Gayle Honeybun
Gayle comes from a very religious family and has an

unnerving habit of kissing the crease every time she goes out to bat. Her ritual seems to pay dividends, however, since Gayle topped the batting averages last season with an aggregate of 109 runs and an average of 7.6.

### 4. Selina Forsyte
Daughter of a former Conservative Party spokesman on Affairs, Selina has endeared herself to fellow players, spectators and umpires during her first full season. She prefers a short cricket skirt to the unisex slacks favoured by many of the other women players. Underneath the skirt she usually wears Teddy Trilling pantiettes and an Arrowsmith Safety Manhole Cover. Selina also pioneered the wearing of the now popular diaphanous cricket blouse. She is learning to throw overarm.

### 5. Maggie Thackeray
The oldest member of the side, Maggie used to be captain until a political upheaval left her out in the cold. After a three year absence from the team she has now won back her place after showing her true form in a series of unusual colour photographs published by one of Kerry Murdock's cricketing magazines.

### 6. Sheila Williams
Unlike Selina Forsyte, Sheila never worries about her appearance and will often go out to bat wearing old gardening clothes. She is a forceful batsperson who always makes her presence felt except on those occasions when she arrives at the wicket too late and is given out by default.

### 7. Julie Halter
Although she has an unfortunate habit of giggling during moments of great tension, Julie is a respected

member of the side. She only recently joined the Shropshire Lasses XI (sponsored by Nusmear Petroleum Jelly) after moving from the London based Vauxhall Virgins Team (sponsored by the Rubber Foundation). Julie has a reputation for catching anything that comes her way. Wicket keeper.

### 8. Pansy Partridge
For four years George Partridge played for the Wykham Wanderers cricket team. It was only when he started to run with his arms flailing and his toes turned in that his team mates guessed he was changing sex. Now George, or Pansy as he is known, is a valuable member of the Shropshire Lasses XI (sponsored by Nusmear Petroleum Jelly). Her habit of eating at least three pounds of raw carrot each day makes her a particularly useful batsperson to send in when the light is bad.

### 9. Barbara Whitehouse
Animal lover, TV pundit and magazine publisher, Barbara Whitehouse still finds time to play cricket once or twice a week. She readily admits that her main value to the team is her ability to remove stains from all sorts of clothing. Grass and red leather stains are her speciality, but few blemishes have been known to resist the Whitehouse Method.

### 10. Suzie Barr
Tiny, small, petite and not very big at all, Suzie Barr has plenty of enthusiasm to make up for her lack of size. Although she still has much to learn about bowling, batting and fielding her skills are much admired.

### 11. Fiona Fulsome
No one has done more for women's cricket than the delectable Fiona Fulsome. She played her first serious game of cricket for the Snowdrop Girls Second XI

when they beat the Folies Bergère first team in the final of the All Paris Women's Cricket Championships in 1944. She was a member of the Saudi Arabia Mixed Team that toured Israel in 1956 and she was vice captain on the Brazilian tour of Mexico in 1980. Her knowledge of the game is vast and although her deafness makes running between the wickets a hazardous procedure for her partners, she remains well worth her place in the side.

# FIVE CRICKETERS OF THE YEAR
*Selected by the Thomas Winsden's Cricketing Almanack Editorial Staff*

### Albert Norman Other (1865– )
For over a century Albert Norman Other has played an important part in cricket matches all around the world. It is impossible to estimate exactly the number of matches he has been involved in during his career, but provisional estimates suggest that during the season which has just ended Albert Norman Other played in at least seven thousand, three hundred and ninety-five. We decided that in appreciation of his steady service to cricket we should place A.N. Other among our five cricketers of the year.

One of the things that has made Albert Norman Other such a noteworthy cricketer has been his ability to vary his style of play to suit the demands of the circumstances. On some occasions, for example, he has startled spectators and other players by the sheer animal force and brute strength of his play.

Never was this aspect of his cricket more noticeable than during last winter when he played in Durban for a local club XI. When Other came in to bat, with eight wickets down and just 43 runs on the board, the prospects looked gloomy for his side. For Albert Norman, however, the challenge was not one to be refused. He immediately set about the bowling with a frightening ferocity. The stroke with which he won the match was, for many of those present, quite unforgettable.

With sparkling footwork, Other drove the ball straight at mid-on who bravely attempted a head high catch. Unfortunately the ball was travelling so fast that it was not so easily stopped. Instead of taking a catch, the hapless fielder found himself being propelled at some 85 mph towards the boundary. When a second or two later, ball and fielder crossed the boundary rope and disappeared into the crowd, the ball was still travelling at head height. It was a six that no one genuinely interested in cricket would have wanted to miss.

On other occasions Albert Norman Other's play has been patchy, to say the least. Take, for example, his performance in another match which took place on the same day several thousand miles away in Sydney, Australia. Other was bowling on an artificial concrete wicket when he delivered a ball so wide that it bounced off the edge of the pitch and disappeared over the head of Third Man. The umpire had no option but to signal six wides.

It would be inappropriate to list the singular achievements of Albert Norman Other without mentioning his remarkable ability to be involved in many different matches at the same time. As an example of his unique skills it should be pointed out that, according to the record books, a ball struck by Other in Kingston, Jamaica was caught at Trent Bridge some three months later by himself! It might be said that no one has done more than Albert Norman Other to bring cricketers around the world closer together.

## Albert Norman Other
### Career Record (estimated)

### Batting

| Matches | Innings | Not outs | Runs | Highest | 100s | Average |
|---------|---------|----------|------|---------|------|---------|
| 648,921 | 845,923 | 128,903 | 23,661,660 | 135 | 174 | 33 |

### Bowling

| Matches | Runs | Wickets | Maidens | Best | Average |
|---------|------|---------|---------|------|---------|
| 648,921 | 444,774 | 13,478 | 5,834 | 5 for 45 | 33 |

### Fielding

| Catches |
|---------|
| 11,926 |

### Wicket Keeping

| Catches | Stumpings |
|---------|-----------|
| 2,347 | 923 |

### Wilhelm Blunderbuss KGB, MP, PhD (1932–82)

Few men have ever matched the achievements of Wilhelm Blunderbuss. At the age of 18 he had acquired a double first in English and Pure Physics at Oxford and at Cambridge respectively. At nineteen he ran for his country in the Olympics, winning a gold medal in the 1500 metres and a silver medal in the marathon. He would have taken the gold medal in the marathon if he hadn't stopped on the way to help a small boy who was trapped in a mine shaft.

In his twentieth year Blunderbuss acquired a PhD in Modern Languages and wrote the two slim volumes of poetry which won him a nomination for the Nobel Prize. He played football for England at centre forward, was middleweight boxing champion of Europe and was elected a Member of Parliament at the age of twenty-two.

On his twenty-fourth birthday, Blunderbuss resigned from the post of Foreign Secretary on a matter of principle. In the same year he made a fortune by bringing aid to underdeveloped countries. For that he was awarded the Nobel Prize for peace at about the same time as his first musical was performed on Broadway.

He added the Wimbledon Tennis Championship to his rowing blue and his Open Golf Championship before he was thirty. Not long afterwards, he married Miss World and wrote his best selling novel about Russian prison camps.

For some men, these achievements would have been enough; for Blunderbuss they were unmemorable events in a life of disappointment. His real ambition remained unfulfilled. From an early age Blunderbuss had wanted nothing more than to score 1000 runs during one cricket season.

Wealth, power, the cheers of the crowd at Wembley, Twickenham and St Andrews, the accolades from the international literary establishment, the contracts pouring in from Hollywood film producers begging for his talents as an actor and director, his hit records and his successes in the Cheltenham Gold Cup, the Derby and the Grand National, were all as nothing to Blunderbuss.

Last year, knowing the nature of the yearning which blazed in Blunderbuss's heart, some of his dearest friends decided to try to help the great man achieve his ambition. Although he was in his fiftieth year, he was still fit and strong and they had little difficulty in persuading a local village side to give him a place as an opening batsman. It was decided that Blunderbuss should open each innings – thereby gaining the greatest possible opportunity of reaching his target.

The season began badly. Although it was his greatest love, cricket was Blunderbuss's Achilles' heel. He had great difficulty in keeping bat and pad together, he never managed to time the ball properly and when he did manage to connect, he invariably hit the ball straight to a fielder.

Despite his natural shortcomings, Blunderbuss did manage to score *sometimes*. By mid-August he had accumulated 853 runs and he looked all set to reach that magic 1000. He didn't much mind what his final average was – the golden aggregate was important. Then he hit a bad patch.

He was dismissed for 0,2,0,1,0,3,0,0,4,0 and 1 in successive innings before the season ended. Blunderbuss had missed his target by a tantalising 136 runs. He was heartbroken.

His friends, however, were not inclined to give up so easily. They arranged three more matches in September. In the first, Blunderbuss managed to accumulate 23 runs. In the second he scored a disappointing 3 and in the third he scored 17. He now needed less than 100 runs.

In the matches which were arranged for October, Blunderbuss scored a total of 45 runs. In the four matches that took place in November, he put together another 28. This meant that by December Blunderbuss needed only 20 runs to reach his 1000. And then it started to snow.

With the target a mere 20 runs away, Blunderbuss's friends were not going to be stopped by a few snowflakes! They told him that the team had been invited to play in a couple of special Christmas matches and assured him that this was all part of a normal season. Throughout September, October and November Blunderbuss had happily accepted that the cricket season continued for as long as the weather remained reasonable. To persuade him that matches played in the snow were a normal part of the season's activities took some ingenuity, but with the aid of a specially-printed copy of *Thomas Winsden's Cricketing Almanack* (in which we were pleased and proud to print details of matches played in snow the previous December) Blunderbuss was finally convinced.

And so it was that on December 31st, after a foot and a half of snow had been brushed away from the batting crease and the spot where a well-pitched ball would land swept clean, Blunderbuss scored the final few runs which took him to his target. Unhappily, the occasion wasn't quite perfect.

Overcome by cold and excitement, Wilhelm Blunderbuss died at the very moment when an over-enthusiastic return from a clumsy fielder gave him the runs he needed for his total. He never knew that he'd achieved his final ambition.

## Wilhelm Blunderbuss
*Career Record*

| Matches | Innings | Not out | Runs | Highest | 10s | Average |
|---------|---------|---------|------|---------|-----|---------|
| 73 | 73 | 0 | 1000 | 49 | 9 | 13.7 |

| Catches |
|---------|
| 1 |

## Reg T.K. Ganter (1933–   )

When Reg Ganter edged a single to third man in the final match of his team's fixture list, the reaction of the crowd came close to hysteria – they knew that Ganter had just become the first Australian in living memory to score a thousand runs in a season without once hitting the ball in the middle of the bat.

Known to friends and enemies alike as 'the luckiest cricketer in the world', Ganter delights his fellow team members, but confounds his critics and opponents, by continuing to collect runs and wickets without ever really showing any signs of knowing what he is doing or understanding the fundamental principles of the game.

For several years now his most successful scoring stroke has been the edged drive, which sends a snick flying over the heads of the slips. Ganter himself will readily admit, however, that the stroke he plays best is the one in which he closes his eyes, puts his left leg firmly down the pitch, swings across the line and then simply runs up and down the wicket until his batting partner suggests that valour give way to discretion.

If Ganter is lucky as a batsman, however, he seems to possess almost supernatural good fortune when bowling. Cricket statistician Ernest Briggs (whose study of Ganter's career accompanies this short biography) claims that Ganter's striking-rate is probably greater than that of any other bowler, living or dead.

If any batsman facing one of Ganter's modest medium-pace deliveries is hit on the pads it seems he is invariably given out lbw. If he hits the ball with his bat then he will almost certainly be caught since the ball always carries directly to a fielder. If a batsman attempts to hit a Ganter delivery for six then in all probability his hat will fall off and dislodge his bails. If two batsmen decide to risk taking runs off Ganter then you can be sure that at least one of them will be run out. Batsmen who have spent hours parrying fierce and frightening deliveries from genuinely fast bowlers will succumb to Ganter's modest and apparently harmless deliveries; batsmen who have failed to be impressed by the efforts of the world's top class spinners always appear completely bamboozled by Ganter's ordinary efforts.

As a fielder Ganter has more than his fair share of luck. As a captain he has learnt to rely on winning the toss and being blessed by the weather. As a cricketer he is a man with severely limited talents but unlimited good fortune. He well deserves his place as one of our five cricketers of the year.

## Reg Ganter's Lifetime Statistical Record
Batting

| Year | Matches | Innings | Not out | Runs | Snicked/Edged | Times dropped | Average |
|------|---------|---------|---------|------|---------------|---------------|---------|
| 1964 | 4 | 5 | 4 | 180 | 163 | 11 | 180 |

| Year | Matches | Innings | Not out | Runs | Snicked/Edged | Times dropped | Average |
|------|---------|---------|---------|------|---------------|---------------|---------|
| 1965 | 7 | 8 | 3 | 218 | 204 | 18 | 40.8 |
| 1966 | 9 | 11 | 5 | 317 | 309 | 28 | 51.12 |
| 1967 | 12 | 17 | 11 | 567 | 564 | 37 | 94.5 |
| 1968 | 12 | 15 | 12 | 643 | 628 | 35 | 214.33 |
| 1969 | 18 | 22 | 17 | 987 | 937 | 46 | 197.4 |
| 1970 | 17 | 21 | 16 | 854 | 837 | 38 | 170.8 |
| 1971 | 19 | 17 | 15 | 749 | 737 | 27 | 374.5 |
| 1972 | 21 | 27 | 22 | 996 | 948 | 57 | 199.2 |
| 1973 | 23 | 22 | 20 | 953 | 925 | 62 | 476.5 |
| 1974 | 19 | 27 | 23 | 845 | 837 | 59 | 211.25 |
| 1975 | 18 | 21 | 20 | 786 | 786 | 67 | 786.0 |
| 1976 | 19 | 23 | 22 | 679 | 678 | 83 | 679.0 |
| 1977 | 25 | 27 | 20 | 752 | 751 | 96 | 107.42 |
| 1978 | 22 | 17 | 14 | 592 | 591 | 86 | 197.33 |
| 1979 | 24 | 27 | 22 | 953 | 952 | 76 | 190.6 |
| 1980 | 27 | 28 | 25 | 947 | 946 | 95 | 315.33 |
| 1981 | 25 | 29 | 26 | 963 | 962 | 93 | 320.66 |
| 1982 | 22 | 27 | 24 | 1000 | 1000 | 98 | 333.33 |

## Reg Ganter
Bowling

| Year | Overs | Mdns | Runs | Appeals | Wickets | Average | Catches dropped |
|------|-------|------|------|---------|---------|---------|-----------------|
| 1964 | 78 | 43 | 103 | 33 | 33 | 3.12 | 0 |
| 1965 | 88 | 37 | 111 | 47 | 47 | 2.36 | 0 |
| 1966 | 94 | 38 | 109 | 56 | 56 | 1.95 | 0 |
| 1967 | 98 | 27 | 117 | 47 | 47 | 2.49 | 0 |
| 1968 | 103 | 67 | 124 | 65 | 65 | 1.91 | 0 |
| 1969 | 108 | 78 | 265 | 98 | 98 | 2.70 | 0 |
| 1970 | 87 | 53 | 104 | 95 | 95 | 1.09 | 0 |
| 1971 | 98 | 46 | 97 | 93 | 93 | 1.04 | 0 |
| 1972 | 176 | 53 | 109 | 102 | 97 | 1.12 | 0 |
| 1973 | 205 | 76 | 117 | 145 | 145 | 0.81 | 0 |
| 1974 | 200 | 86 | 193 | 125 | 125 | 1.54 | 0 |
| 1975 | 387 | 116 | 204 | 112 | 111 | 1.84 | 0 |
| 1976 | 108 | 92 | 87 | 119 | 119 | 0.73 | 0 |
| 1977 | 276 | 108 | 187 | 196 | 195 | 0.96 | 1 |
| 1978 | 250 | 92 | 276 | 290 | 289 | 0.95 | 0 |
| 1979 | 276 | 83 | 387 | 202 | 202 | 1.92 | 0 |
| 1980 | 269 | 69 | 276 | 178 | 178 | 1.55 | 0 |
| 1981 | 670 | 264 | 548 | 367 | 367 | 1.49 | 0 |
| 1982 | 543 | 387 | 643 | 328 | 328 | 1.18 | 0 |

## Reg Ganter
Captaincy

| Year | Toss won | Times own innings interrupted by rain | Times opponents' innings interrupted by rain |
|------|----------|----------------------------------------|-----------------------------------------------|
| 1981 | 98% | 2 | 27 |
| 1982 | 100% | 0 | 33 |

## Nelson Plunge (1927–    )

When the editors and cricket advisers here at *Thomas Winsden's Cricketing Almanack* were considering candidates for this feature, one name kept recurring: that of Nelson Plunge, for twenty-five years a mainstay of the Crown and Anchor team in the village of Wyre Puddle.

It would be wrong to pretend that Plunge could have been a candidate for international honours. Equally, it would be unrealistic to suggest that he was unlucky not to play for his county side and inaccurate to say that he deserved his place in the Crown and Anchor team.

Whatever criticisms one might make of Plunge's cricketing skills, however, his value as a team member and cricket enthusiast could not be over-emphasised. When the nettles on the boundary edge became a threat, it was Plunge who trimmed them. When the pitch needed rolling it was Plunge who found the roller, oiled it and undertook the task. When the grass had to be cut it was Plunge who came to the rescue – regardless of the fact that the lead on his Hovermower reached only half-way to the wicket. When the crease marks wore off halfway through the season, it was Plunge who found some more pump-whitener to freshen them.

If an umpire didn't turn up, Plunge it was who would don a white coat and officiate, selflessly ignoring his allegiance to the Crown and Anchor team and bravely forgetting his almost total ignorance of the laws of cricket.

When one of the team's stumps was broken in 1957,

who made a replacement out of a chair leg? Plunge. When the bails were lost during the horseplay which followed a rare victory in 1959 it was Plunge again, who made a spare set out of the remains of that very same chair. When the team's ball was lost in 1960 Plunge was the saviour once more; spending a day and a half knee deep in the local stream, he finally located a ball that had been lost there in 1958.

When the team went on tour to Cheshire and Devon in 1963, and only five members turned up to join the minibus, Plunge bravely took on the role of captain. He managed to recruit fresh players from the villages and clubs they had arranged to play and was so successful that when the minibus returned to the Crown and Anchor there were fourteen players in the party.

Nelson Plunge may not have set the world on fire with his cricketing skills, but he was, and is, a genuine afficianado, an archetypal cricket fan and a real friend to the game he loves so much. We congratulate him on his selection as one of our Cricketers of the Year.

## Nelson Plunge
### Career Record

Batting

| Year | Matches | Innings | Runs | Not outs | Highest | Average |
|------|---------|---------|------|----------|---------|---------|
| 1956 | 4 | 2 | 3 | 0 | 2 | 1.5 |
| 1957 | 6 | 3 | 4 | 0 | 2 | 1.3 |
| 1958 | 11 | 5 | 10 | 2 | 3 | 1.6 |
| 1959 | 14 | 7 | 9 | 3 | 2 | 2.25 |
| 1960 | 5 | 1 | 0 | 0 | 0 | 0 |
| 1961 | 1 | 0 | 0 | 0 | 0 | 0 |
| 1962 | 12 | 10 | 24 | 0 | 6 | 2.4 |
| 1963 | 14 | 6 | 10 | 1 | 3 | 2 |
| 1964 | 11 | 3 | 5 | 0 | 5 | 1.66 |
| 1965 | 1 | 1 | 1 | 0 | 1 | 1 |
| 1966 | 2 | 1 | 0 | 0 | 0 | 0 |
| 1967 | 1 | 1 | 7 | 0 | 7 | 7 |
| 1968 | 15 | 10 | 14 | 0 | 4 | 1.4 |
| 1969 | 12 | 8 | 19 | 1 | 2 | 2.71 |
| 1970 | 3 | 1 | 2 | 0 | 2 | 2 |

| Year | Matches | Innings | Runs | Not outs | Highest | Average |
|------|---------|---------|------|----------|---------|---------|
| 1971 | 11 | 10 | 22 | 0 | 4 | 2.2 |
| 1972 | 14 | 8 | 17 | 1 | 3 | 2.42 |
| 1973 | 12 | 9 | 22 | 0 | 5 | 2.44 |
| 1974 | 11 | 7 | 18 | 1 | 3 | 3 |
| 1975 | 12 | 7 | 22 | 0 | 4 | 3.14 |
| 1976 | 11 | 6 | 15 | 0 | 3 | 2.5 |
| 1977 | 1 | 0 | 0 | 0 | 0 | 0 |
| 1978 | 1 | 1 | 3 | 0 | 3 | 3 |
| 1979 | 10 | 6 | 27 | 1 | 7 | 5.4 |
| 1980 | 15 | 12 | 22 | 1 | 4 | 2 |
| 1981 | 14 | 9 | 25 | 0 | 4 | 2.77 |
| 1982 | 14 | 8 | 17 | 1 | 5 | 2.43 |
| Total | 238 | 142 | 318 | 12 | 7 | 2.45 |

## Bowling (years when available)

| Year | Overs | Maidens | Runs | Wickets | Average |
|------|-------|---------|------|---------|---------|
| 1958 | 3 | 0 | 8 | 0 | - |
| 1963 | 4 | 1 | 37 | 0 | - |
| 1969 | 6 | 1 | 67 | 0 | - |
| 1975 | 3 | 0 | 34 | 1 | 34 |
| 1976 | 67 | 1 | 276 | 1 | 276 |
| 1981 | 3 | 0 | 7 | 0 | - |
| 1982 | 1 | 0 | 13 | 0 | - |

***Note from the Production Director.***
Although this section is headed *Five Cricketers of the Year*, there was only copy for Four Cricketers of the Year. I take no responsibility for this. I made many attempts to telephone the editorial offices of the *Almanack*, but, as usual, there was no reply. Finally I could delay no longer because the book had to be printed and I'm putting in this note just to make it clear that it isn't my responsibility and I'm not taking any blame.

# UMPIRES' AVERAGES FOR THE 1982 SEASON

Once again the umpires' averages make fascinating reading. Batsmen won't be surprised to see that Andy Turner and Nigel Mohr are both well down the list as far as dismissals per innings are concerned. For the fourteenth time in a career spanning fifteen seasons, Mohr dismissed an average of less than half a batsman per innings.

At the other end of the scale, 'Fingers' Kray's belligerence was once again in evidence. With a record-breaking average of 9.89 dismissals per innings, Kray is the umpire all batsmen hope to avoid. Many batsmen are waiting to see whether Kray's younger brother, joining the umpires list this year for the first time, will be as harsh.

'Fingers' Kray also tops the appeals/wicket table with a remarkable record of 1.003. In practical terms this means that every time a bowler appeals to umpire Kray he gets a wicket. Bottom of the table is Nigel Mohr again – this time with a differential of 8.65.

## Umpires averages for last season: leading figures for umpires in all classes of cricket

| Name | Matches | Innings | Appeals | Bowled | Caught |
|------|---------|---------|---------|--------|--------|
| Fingers Kray | 32 | 55 | 546 | 128 | 8 |
| E.Z. Connor | 27 | 48 | 348 | 101 | 42 |
| Bails Orf | 30 | 49 | 193 | 3 | 28 |
| M.I. Blinde | 28 | 52 | 928 | 29 | 58 |
| A. Turner | 30 | 55 | 745 | 83 | 11 |
| N.E. Mohr | 27 | 43 | 128 | 6 | 3 |
| Noddy Kopf | 26 | 49 | 458 | 10 | 0 |

continued:-

| Run out | LBW | Hit wkt | Stumped | The Rest | Total | Average/ innings | Appeals/ wkt |
|---------|-----|---------|---------|----------|-------|------------------|--------------|
| 96 | 245 | 11 | 19 | 37 | 544 | 9.89 | 1.003 |
| 0 | 147 | 0 | 0 | 0 | 290 | 6.04 | 1.20 |
| 7 | 40 | 2 | 0 | 0 | 80 | 1.6 | 2.39 |
| 57 | 66 | 6 | 0 | 30 | 244 | 4.69 | 3.80 |
| 5 | 57 | 0 | 3 | 0 | 159 | 2.89 | 4.67 |
| 0 | 0 | 0 | 6 | 0 | 15 | 0.34 | 8.65 |

*Note*
'The Rest' includes batsmen dismissed: obstructed the field, hit the ball twice and handled the ball.

# SANDWICH MAKERS' AVERAGES

Yet again the sandwich makers' table has been topped by an egg and cress specialist. It seems you just can't beat egg and cress if you want good figures at the end of the season! Last year it was Mrs Knuttall who won the golden knife award. This year, Mrs Knuttall was out of the reckoning with a broken left wrist and Doris Pettifer took her chance with both hands. She cut and buttered for 36 matches, made a total of 1582 sandwiches and saw only 59 of them go to waste. With 1523 eaten she had an average of 42.3 sandwiches eaten per match. That's nearly one and a half sandwiches more than the record Mrs Knuttall set in 1977.

Of the newcomers, Kathy Hawks – a cheese and tomato specialist – looked particularly promising. She'd never cut and buttered for a cricket team before but her work with her boyfriend's XI won her fifth place on this year's table of merit.

A word of commendation, too, for Nora Asquith, the only non-specialist in the top five to have been a sandwich maker for more than thirty years. Nora's ham, cheese and tomato sandwiches have fed cricketers all around the world. Sadly, this is to be her last season. We wish her well.

# SANDWICH MAKERS' AVERAGES – VILLAGE LEAGUE CRICKET

| Name | Matches | S'wiches made | No. eaten | Highest | 100s | Average |
|------|---------|---------------|-----------|---------|------|---------|
| Mrs Pettifer (E & C) | 36 | 1582 | 1523 | 112 | 2 | 42.3 |
| Mrs Thatcher (C, H) | 32 | 1547 | 1309 | 102 | 1 | 40.9 |
| Mrs Asquith (H, C & T) | 17 | 987 | 678 | 114 | 2 | 39.9 |
| Mrs Pynchon (C) | 19 | 736 | 735 | 98 | 0 | 38.7 |
| Miss Hawks (C & T) | 24 | 1025 | 902 | 67 | 0 | 37.6 |
| Mrs Windsor (H) | 11 | 954 | 411 | 98 | 0 | 37.4 |
| Mrs Castle (C) | 32 | 1986* | 1181 | 143 | 3 | 36.9 |
| Mrs Swansdown (H) | 24 | 1543 | 881 | 123 | 2 | 36.7 |
| Miss Jelks (C, C & T) | 19 | 646 | 646 | 116 | 2 | 34.0 |
| Miss Condor (H) | 29 | 1176 | 966 | 124 | 3 | 33.3 |
| Mrs Rantzen (C) | 37 | 1832 | 1180 | 109 | 4 | 31.9 |
| Mrs Rippon (C & T) | 6 | 193 | 178 | 52 | 0 | 29.6 |
| Miss Dodds (C & T) | 14 | 562 | 343 | 75 | 0 | 24.5 |
| Mrs Oaks (H) | 27 | 739 | 613 | 100 | 1 | 22.7 |
| Mrs Forsyth (H, C) | 22 | 638 | 464 | 53 | 0 | 21.1 |
| Mrs Ford (C & T) | 21 | 937 | 407 | 41 | 0 | 19.4 |
| Mrs Barton (H, C & T) | 33 | 1738 | 112 | 17 | 0 | 3.4 |
| Mrs Penn (H) | 18 | 937 | 47 | 8 | 0 | 2.6 |
| Mrs Taylor (C) | 22 | 749 | 31 | 3 | 0 | 1.4 |
| Mrs Healey (C) | 28 | 237 | 25 | 4 | 0 | 0.9 |

## Notes

1
E & C – egg and cress specialist
C & T – cheese and tomato specialist
C     – cheese secialist
H     – ham specialist

2
The average in the final column represents the number of sandwiches consumed per match.

3
*includes sixteen sandwiches later found to have contained meat infested with salmonella.

# General features

## THE INSTANT CRICKET CUP

This year a new competition will be launched in South Africa. – specially designed to attract those who stay away from cricket matches because they dislike the notion of having to watch a game that lasts for half a day – or even longer.

Known as the Ninety Minute Cup, the new competition was devised by those brilliant minds that gave us television's popular game shows, *What's My Game?*, *Game for a Grin* and *The Ingratiation Game*.

Each side competing in the Cup will be allowed to bat for no more than eleven overs, with each batsman facing the whole of one six ball over. At the end of the eleven overs, the number of runs the eleven batsmen have scored will be known as the First Team's Total Number of Runs. The number of times that all the batsmen have been given out will also be added up and will represent the First Team's Total Number of Dismissals.

Working with the aid of a XZQ 5000 computer, a team of skilled and dedicated scientists will then work out the average number of runs that have been scored for each dismissal. The result will be known as the First Team's Average Score.

After a short break to give everyone time to recover from the excitement, the bowling side will then become the batting side and the batting side will become the bowling side. To make things less confusing for specta-tors, the batsmen will always wear blue while the bowlers will always wear green.

Each of the eleven overs must be bowled by a differ-ent member of the side but, once again, the scorers will add up the total number of runs per batsman and the total number of times that each batsman is dismissed. And, again, at the end of the innings, that marvellous XZQ 5000 computer and the team of scientists will work out the Second Team's Average Score. By then there will be no secret about the winner. It will be the side that has the highest Average Score.

Two more things to remember are that batsmen must hop between the wickets and that bowlers must deliver after a hop, step and jump run-up. All the leading cric-ket stars are said to be looking forward to the new competition.

# USEFUL TIPS FOR WOMEN CRICKETERS

More and more women are taking to cricket, though many are new recruits and have never played before. Conscious of the needs of these players, we have pre-pared a series of basic hints for noviciates.

1.   If you play in a skirt, do be careful when buckling your pads. It is all too easy to get a fold of skin caught in the buckle and disfiguring bruising can result.
2.   Polishing the ball with lip gloss is considered to be unfair play.
3.   Pregnant wicket keepers should stand well back from the stumps – particularly if the bowler is above medium pace. When keeping for a fast bowler, the pregnant wicket keeper should stand just inside the boundary rope.

4. If you're handy with a needle and thread, you'll be able to make your own pads. Do remember, however, that you may need to bat in the rain and make sure that they are constructed from a shrinkproof material.

5. Remember that some parts of the human body are more vulnerable than others. Toxteth's Little Nipple Guards are a must for all women playing cricket.

6. When you're batting you'll need to run between the wickets if either you or your partner manages to hit the ball. Practice running without flinging your arms out to the side. If you run like that when you've got a bat in your hand, you might cause injury to a slips or gully fielder.

7. Do remember that in any team there will usually be two or three players who are pre-menstrual. If a bowler bursts into tears because an appeal is turned down, or a batsperson returns to the pavilion in obvious distress, then do try to be sympathetic. A cuddle and a smile can work wonders.

8. Learn to bend at the knees when picking up a ball. This is particularly important if you're likely to be in the outfield. Some experienced women cricketers spend a little time at the start of each season practising looks of disdain.

9. In mixed cricket it is considered unsporting for a woman favouring a short skirt to wear stockings and suspenders. It's also bad form to have more than one blouse button undone.

10. Woolly bat-handles help to keep your hands warm; they look attractive too. Try to make sure that all the members of your team choose the same colour. Nothing looks worse than two batspersons with different coloured bat-handle covers! You can obtain a knitting pattern for a bat cover, ball cosy and stump sheath by writing to the *Thomas Winsden's Cricketing Almanack* offices. Please send a stamped, addressed envelope and details of your preferred needlesize.

## Joker is wild

A practical joker changed the signs on the Beer Tent and the First Aid Tent at the Hastings Festival Match last year.

The 'joke' was only noticed at the end of the day, by which time two St. John's Ambulance men had examined and bandaged 17,593 spectators. Sixty thousand gallons of warm beer had to be thrown away.

## Umpires

The first class umpires list for the coming season will include ex-Superintendent Richardson and ex-Inspector Kray, both formerly of the Metropolitan Police Force (Traffic Division). Neither men have any previous experience of cricket or of umpiring but both have long arms, some knowledge of bumpers and have studied the effects of damp surfaces on velocity.

## No-Noise Bat Banned

In June, the Test and Country Cricket Board announced that Arrowsmith's Noiseless Bat was to be banned from use in competitive cricket.

The bat, made from ordinary seasoned willow but coated with a special non-resinate polymer, had become extremely popular with batsmen because the special coating ensured that contact between bat and ball was completely silent.

During the three months that the bat was used in competitive cricket, the number of catches taken by wicket-keepers and slips had fallen by between 85% and 90%.

To effect the ban the games administrators invoked rule 79c which states 'The administrators may at any time and without warning change, alter, revoke, or expand any rule whether it already exists or not.'

# ON BEING A CAPTAIN

In an attempt to help readers to learn the rudiments of captaincy quickly and painlessly, we spoke at some length to Mr Aubrey Beadsley who, during his years as captain of the Princetown XI impressed members, players and spectators with his understanding of the needs and expectations of his players. With Mr. Beadsley's help we have prepared the following short-list of tips for potential captains.

1. You must try to be consistent. Your players will feel cheated if you always insist on opening the batting when the opposition's bowling is weak, but prefer to bat at number 10 or 11 when the other team possesses a genuinely quick bowler. Your fellow players will be similarly discouraged if you bowl only when the opposition's batting is weak but always take yourself off when your own bowling attack is being torn apart.

2. Always win the toss. Even if you lose you should tell your players that you won. It is better that they think your decisions eccentric than that you are an unlucky captain.

3. Try to be tactful when offering advice to players. When one of your batsmen has been dismissed, wait at least five minutes before telling him what he did wrong and why his thoughtlessness has upset you.

4. Don't be tempted to rush about when your side is fielding. Your job is to stand at mid-on (or possibly mid-off) and try to keep an overall view of the game. If you're constantly chasing balls to the boundary, you'll get hot and sticky and won't be in a fit state to make important decisions.

5. Do offer encouragement to your players whenever you think it is appropriate. Don't be afraid to tell them that you're pleased when they do something particularly impressive. A quick burst of applause from the balcony

or from mid-on will do nicely. You can add an extra ice cube to their drinks at the next interval if you like. Let them see you smile and if they do something really marvellous let them call you by your first name for the rest of the day.

6.  Always be adaptable and ready to lend a helping hand. As captain you should be prepared to supervise the rolling of the wicket, the varnishing of the stumps, the finding of the ball and the preparation of the sandwiches. You should also be available to offer consolation to the wives of your players if they are made lonely by the absences of their husbands during the season.

7.  Players can sometimes be touchy, demanding, ungrateful, suspicious and sensitive. Some of the members of your team will resent your authority and be jealous of your status and success. Explain to them that if they are prepared to work hard, improve their standards of play and mature a little, then they too may one day achieve captaincy. They will be eternally grateful to you.

+++

### International Club Cricket Conference gets the runaround!

In May last year the International Club Cricket Conference announced that bowlers in first-, second- and third-class cricket matches must, in future, limit themselves to a run up of twenty-five yards.

Unfortunately, the administrator who prepared the relevant legislation merely said that bowlers could not begin their run ups more than twenty-five yards away from the popping crease and within a month of the new rule's enforcement, many bowlers were running round in circles in order to build up extra speed. Batsmen, umpires and bowlers themselves found this confusing and disturbing. At least one bowler fell over on the way in to deliver the ball.

The International Club Cricket Conference will be

meeting next June to discuss ways in which bowlers can be forced to approach the wicket in a straight line.

# THE GREATEST TOURS

### No. 17: The Germans in France 1916

Only once have German cricketers toured France. Partly because of the unique nature of this tour, and partly because the tour took place in the summer of 1916, the visit has fascinated cricket researchers and historians for many years. Other events in Europe at that time tended to overshadow the tour and because sports editors were having to make do with severely reduced space, contemporary newspapers and periodicals included very few reports of the matches played.

During the last twelve months, however, investigating historians have come across diaries and old score books which give a more detailed picture of the tour than has ever been available.

The new evidence suggests that the German tourists were first invited to tour France in 1913, probably via Belgium. Despite suggestions from Berlin that they consider the possibility of cancelling at least part of the tour, the German cricketers insisted that the game came above such incidental hazards and inconveniences as might be posed by a mere war.

Some writers have expressed surprise that the tour should have gained approval from the French, but modern historians now believe that although many of those responsible did have grave misgivings about the wisdom of allowing the matches to be played, pressure was brought to bear from the overseas committee of the Marylebone Cricket Club. Few Governments can resist that sort of pressure.

A full account of the tour is contained in a new book entitled *The Germans in France in 1916*, written by

R.T. Chere and published by Shoulderarms Press. The book contains a full statistical account of the tour and Shoulderarms Press have kindly given us permission to reproduce in *Thomas Winsden's Cricketing Almanack* the statistical summary with which the book ends.

### *Statistical summary for Germans in France 1916*

|  |  |  |  | Tourists | | Home teams | |
|---|---|---|---|---|---|---|---|
| *Matches played* | *Won* | *Lost* | *Drawn* | *Killed* | *Injured* | *Killed* | *Injured* |
| 13 | 3 | 2 | 8 | 6 | 4 | 7 | 2 |

---

**University Blues 1982**
Several university players suffered from 'the blues' in 1982 but R. Russell Smith (reading neurocomputer sciences at Derby University) had more reason than most to suffer from depression.

In the friendly matches at the start of the season he scored more runs and took more wickets than any other player but, after spending the weekend in Amersham with the captain's girl friend, lost his place in the side. As a consequence, he suffered from 'the blues' all season.

---

# GUIDELINES FOR COMFORTABLE SPECTATING

Many people attend cricket matches only rarely. As a result of their inexperience, they simply don't know what to take in the way of equipment, refreshment and so forth.

It's important to get this sort of paraphernalia right in order to avoid social embarassment. In an attempt to help the less-knowledgeable visitor, Marylebone Cricket Club's tourist and spectator committee has published a series of guidelines for 'comfortable spectating'. With their permission we reproduce these suggestions here.

### For spectating in public enclosures
A bright red or yellow anorak with a hood attached.

If you want to wear a sun hat, then take a floppy, white one. If you forget your hat you can usually obtain a rather nice cardboard eyeshade from one of the sponsors' tents.

A blue ballpoint pen for filling in your score-card. (You will have to purchase your score-card when you arrive at the ground. These are very cheap and good value.)

Twelve cans of beer, held together with strips of plastic for easier carrying.

A cheese sandwich wrapped in greaseproof paper and carried in a plastic box.

A small thermos flask filled with coffee that you have milked and sugared to your taste.

An apple. (This can be placed in the plastic box together with your cheese sandwich).

A radio to enable you and your friends to listen to the commentary and find out what is going on.

Money in case your supply of beer runs out.


### For spectators in private or members' enclosures
A golf umbrella or an umbrella in the MCC colours.

A pair of sunglasses (the sort that react to light not the polarised kind).

A slim gold propelling pencil for filling in your score card.

A pair of binoculars with several torn tickets attached to the neck strap. These tickets should have been obtained at Ascot, Flemington or Cheltenham.

A small pocket-sized radio which is fitted with an ear piece. This will enable you to listen to the commentary and find out what is going on without your neighbours knowing what you're doing. Because the commentators have access to TV replay facilities, you will be able to impress those around you by saying things like, 'I rather think that was lbw not caught behind. I think you'll find that the scoreboard will catch on in a minute or two', or 'The scorers are a little slow today. They've given batsman number 3 one run too many. Probably because poor old Joe isn't here. I bet they'll be glad when his rheumatism gets better.' If you use the earpiece ploy, do remember to pretend to be deaf when talking to people.

A small blow up cushion. (Made of canvas, not plastic).

A copy of *Thomas Winsden's Cricketing Almanack* which should be battered and covered with lots of tiny, indecipherable scribbling.

A daily newspaper folded open at the crossword page. The crossword should always be half-completed, though it doesn't matter too much whether or not you have answered the clues correctly.

A wicker covered ice-box which contains the following items:

1. Six quails eggs. (Not necessarily from six quails).
2. Half a French loaf. Small brown loaf. One pound of English butter.
3. Four sorts of cheese – each in a little wooden box. Must include Stilton.
4. A large thermos flask filled with asparagus soup.
5. A bowl, two plates, a cup and saucer and a large collection of silver cutlery. The crockery should all be plain white china.
6. Three long stemmed wine glasses. (Cut glass is not acceptable).
7. A small tub of caviar.
8. Three varieties of paté, each wrapped in a white linen napkin.
9. A large red and white checked napkin for yourself.
10. Twelve oysters packed in an individual ice box, with fresh lemon.
11. Two chicken legs.
12. Two varieties of German sausage.

13. An assortment of cold meats (pork, lamb, beef and tongue but *not* ham).
14. A meringue.
15. A punnet of strawberries with the little green bits still attached.
16. A pot of fresh Devon cream. (It *must* be from Devon).
17. A bottle of good, but not ostentatious, Champagne.
18. A bottle of Chablis.
19. A bottle of St. Emilion.
20. A bottle of port. 1945 is an acceptable year for this sort of occasion.

The contents described above should be suitable for one spectator. For more spectators, multiply accord ingly.

### *The clap made easy – a lesson in simple spectating*
On our visits to cricket grounds last summer we were surprised to find that many spectators still don't know how to clap properly. We have, therefore, prepared a simple guide to this essential spectatorly attribute.

1. Never attempt to clap if you have a glass in one or in both hands. It is considered quite acceptable to restrict yourself to murmurs of 'Good shot' or 'Well played' under the circumstances.

2. If you are uncertain about when to clap, keep an eye on the pavilion and follow the lead of the old men sitting near the players' entrance. They tend to be fairly sparing with their applause because arthritis makes every movement a battle between pleasure and pain; even so it's much better to clap too little than too much.

3. Begin every burst of clapping with a few tentative, token movements. You can always build up to a crescendo if everyone else is applauding heartily but it can be difficult to retain credibility if you appear invariably over-enthusiastic.

4. If you have had too much to drink, keep your elbows tucked into your sides. This will help ensure that your hands actually meet in mid-movement.

5. Remember that it is easier to clap in the vertical plane than in the horizontal. If you suffer from a disease that affects your ability to coordinate muscle movements, then you will find clapping much easier if you leave one hand resting on your lap, palm upwards, and move the other hand gently up and down in a vertical plane.

6. If you find all forms of two-handed clapping impossible to master, then try tapping one hand on your thigh. This is a technique often favoured by the elderly, the infirm and the totally inebriated.

7. Don't stand up when clapping unless you are completely sober.

## ETIQUETTE FOR SPECTATORS

The Marylebone Cricket Club, the Durban & Natal Cricketing Board and the National Playing Fields Association have joined together to produce a charter for spectators. Its rules are designed to ensure that certain standards of behaviour are met.

1. Spectators intending to strip to the waist must pass a 'Fitness for vision' test. The gatemen at each ground will have authority to refuse 'Fitness for vision' certificates to those individuals whom they consider physically unattractive. In general, male spectators will not be allowed to strip to the waist unless they have chest measurements which exceed their waist measurements. Female spectators will not be allowed to strip if their chest measurements are greater than 38 inches (or 36 inches if they intend to stand up and wave their arms about).

2.   No spectator shall throw a beer or cola can in the direction of a player or other spectator unless he has first made sure that the can is empty. Each spectator will have the responsibility for ensuring that the cans he throws have been properly emptied.

3.   Spectators intending to make a noise by banging two cans together shall observe a five minute silence in every twenty minutes. There will be at least thirty minutes silence during every session of play.

4.   Any spectator who runs onto the pitch will return directly to his seat after patting on the back a maximum of two players. He will allow himself to be quietly arrested and will take his punishment like a man. (Or woman as the case may be).

5.   Spectators sitting or standing near the boundary edge will take care at all times to not cover or partially cover advertising hoardings.

6.   Similarly, spectators carrying or waving banners or flags will make sure that they do not cover up any advertising matter.

7.   Any spectator sitting or standing near a television camera will confine his idiotic waving and grinning to times when nothing much is happening.

8.   Spectators intending to streak will consult first with the ground authorities in order to ensure that they choose an appropriate moment. No more than two streakers will be allowed in any one day's play and streakers must make written application for permission to appear on the field. Applications should be accompanied by photographs taken from all angles. (In the case of female streakers these photographs should be in colour).

9.   Spectators shouting advice or rude comments to the players shall do so loudly and clearly.

10. Spectators running onto the pitch at the end of a match will be restricted to taking no more than one stump or one bail.

11. Spectators should not ask for autographs while the bowler is running up to the wicket. Batsmen should not be asked for autographs until they have completed their strokes.

---

**Cricket in Argentina 1982–3**
For the 132nd consecutive year there was no cricket in Argentina.

---

# FOOD AND DRINK FOR THE CRICKETER

More and more cricketers are eating and drinking these days. In order to help those with little experience of catering we have included some simple advice in this edition of *Thomas Winsden's Cricketing Almanack.*

### *How to make a drink of orange squash (for one cricketer)*
Find a glass
Buy a bottle of orange squash
Find a tap
Put a splash of orange squash into the bottom of the glass (you will have to experiment to find the right amount)
Fill the glass with water
That's all there is to it! Good luck!

### *How to make a drink of orange squash (lots of cricketers)*
Find lots of glasses
Buy one (or perhaps two) bottles of orange squash
Find a tap
Put a splash of orange squash into the bottom of each glass
Fill each glass with water.
That's all there is to it! Good luck!

### How to make a drink of lemon squash (for one cricketer)

Find a glass

Buy a bottle of lemon squash

Find a tap

Put a splash of lemon squash into the bottom of the glass (you will have to experiment to find the right amount)

Fill the glass with water

That's all there is to it! Good luck!

### How to make a drink of lemon squash (lots of cricketers)

Find lots of glasses

Buy one (or perhaps two) bottles of lemon squash

Find a tap

Put a splash of lemon squash into the bottom of each glass

Fill the glasses with water

That's all there is to it! Good luck!

### How to make a drink of mixed orange and lemon squash (for one cricketer)

Find a glass

Buy a bottle of orange squash and one bottle of lemon squash

Find a tap

Put half a splash of orange squash into the bottom of the glass

Put half a splash of lemon squash into the bottom of the glass

Fill the glass with water

That's all there is to it! Good luck!

### How to make a drink of mixed orange and lemon squash (lots of cricketers)

Find lots of glasses

Buy one (or perhaps two) bottles of orange squash and
one (or perhaps two) bottles of lemon squash
Find a tap
Put half a splash of orange squash into the bottom of
each glass
Put half a splash of lemon squash into the bottom of
each glass
Fill the glasses with water
That's all there is to it! Good luck!

### How to make a cheese sandwich
Buy a loaf of sliced bread (from a bakery)
Buy a tub of margarine (easier to spread than butter –
ask at the bakery where you can buy some of this)
Buy a hunk of ordinary cheese (cricketers don't like
funny French or Swiss cheeses – ask at the place where
you bought the margarine where you can buy cheese)
Find a knife
Cut the cheese up with the knife. The slices should be
fairly thin. About this thin
Put one piece of bread onto something flat
Smear margarine onto the bread
Put slices of cheese onto the bread until you can't see it
(the bread that is)
Put another slice of bread on top of the cheese
Serve on a plate.

### How to make a cheese and tomato sandwich (this is not recommended for beginners)
Buy a loaf of sliced bread
Buy a tub of margarine
Buy a hunk of ordinary cheese
Buy a tomato
Find a knife
Cut the cheese up with the knife
Put one piece of bread on something flat
Smear margarine onto the bread

Put slices of cheese onto the bread until you cannot see it
Now place the tomato on top of the cheese
Quickly put another slice of bread on top of the tomato on top of the cheese
Press down very hard
Serve on a plate.

## *Making a cup of coffee*
Buy a jar of 'instant' coffee
Find a spoon
Find a cup or mug
Find a kettle
Find a tap
Find a heat source (gas, electricity or lots of candles)
Put a spoonful of coffee into the cup or mug
Fill the kettle with water from the tap
Heat the kettle (the water will get hot automatically)
When the kettle is very hot pour some of the water into the cup
You now have a cup of black coffee
If you want a cup of white coffee you must find some milk. You must then pour some of the milk into the coffee so that it goes brown. (White coffee is actually brown, not white)
If you want sugar in your coffee you must also find some sugar and a teaspoon
Scoop up one (or two, or three) spoonfuls of sugar and put them into the coffee
Stir until the sugar has dissolved
It is much easier to drink it black and unsweetened.

## *Making a cup of tea*
Buy a tea bag
Find a cup or mug
Find a kettle
Find a tap

Find a heat source (gas, electricity or lots of candles)
Put the tea bag into the cup or mug
Heat the kettle
When the kettle is very hot pour some of the water into the cup
Wait a minute or two
Now take the tea bag out of the cup or mug
If you want milk in your tea you must borrow some
Find a person who has made white coffee and borrow milk from him
He may be able to lend you sugar (if you want sugar in your tea) and a teaspoon. Scoop up one (or two, or three) spoonfuls of sugar and put them into the tea. Stir until the sugar has dissolved.

### Serving cakes and buns
Buy some cakes and buns
Put them on a plate
Serve them to people
Wash the plate.


# THE TWELFTH MAN'S DUTIES

### Hints and Tips for Beginners
1.  Always look smart. Wear newly-pressed flannels and clean boots. Make sure that your flannels and your shirt are a similar shade of white.
2.  If you are going out to field, step onto the grass gingerly. Walk, don't run, to your appointed position. Try to be as inconspicuous as possible.
3.  When fielding, be neat and effective but never obtrusive. The player whose position you have taken will never forgive you if you seem to be better at his work than he.
4.  When leaving the field try to do so without fuss. Don't wave to spectators as you leave and don't sign

autographs as you saunter up the pavilion steps.

5.   Always wear a blazer when taking out the drinks. The blazer must be dark blue and should have a large badge or crest on the breast pocket. The middle button must be fastened. Do not have pens or pencils on display in your blazer pocket.

6.   The tray should be carried in both hands. Grip the sides of the tray firmly with the thumbs pointing in the direction in which you are going. (Make sure that your thumb and finger nails are neatly trimmed).

7.   Never fill glasses to the top. If you do you'll spill fluid onto the tray. It's not a pleasant sight and apart from that is considered horribly infra dig.

8.   There should be fifteen glasses on the tray: one for each fielder, one for each batsman and one for each umpire. A good mix is to have five glasses filled with orange squash, five with lemon squash and five with lime cordial.

9.   If you know that one of the players (or umpires) always likes a tot of something in his drink then mark that glass with a straw. In the excitement of taking out the drinks it is all too easy to forget and give the special drink to the wrong person. This can cause problems.

10.  Collect together *all* the glasses before you bring the tray back to the pavilion. It is bad manners to expect a player to have to run after you with his glass.

11.  If you carry a pitcher full of extra fluid on your tray make sure that it contains enough ice cubes for all the players (and umpires). No-one should be allowed to take two ice cubes. You can use a tea strainer to help you ration out the ice cubes. Keep the tea strainer in your trouser pocket so that it does not spoil the line of your jacket or blazer.

12.  When you carry the tray back to the pavilion your hands must grip the tray firmly and your thumbs point in the direction in which you are walking.

# "W.G. GRACE NOT W.G. GRACE AT ALL" SAYS STATISTICIAN!

*Shock revelation from leading cricket writer*

In a startling lecture at the Uterhouse Cricket Society's Annual Specificity Meeting (at which, by tradition, cricket observers and statisticians are invited to give papers dealing with very special topics of interest) the well known cricket writer Percy Pointer claimed that the batting and bowling averages usually attributed to the late, great Dr. W.G. Grace belong to a little-known player called Francis Bacon.

First rebutting a previous claim that Grace's statistics had been the result of the skill of another minor cricketer, Christopher Marlowe, Pointer went on to explain that Grace himself had been a far from enthusiastic cricketer. Most of his sporting career was devoted to croquet, claimed Pointer, and the muddle concerning the averages had arisen out of a confusion between the two games.

According to the research work Pointer has done, W.G. Grace himself played only in two cricket matches – both of them while he was still at school. In one match he batted twice, scoring 11 and 3, and bowled 12 overs to take 2 wickets for 87 runs. In the second match he batted once and scored 17 but did not bowl at all.

To prove his case Mr Pointer made the following observations:

1. Both W.G. Grace and Francis Bacon lived at approximately the same time.
2. Both men had beards.
3. Neither man ever met Queen Victoria.
4. Both were connected with the medical profession. W.G. Grace was a physician while Francis Bacon had a nephew who worked in a chemist's shop in Shrewsbury.
5. Both men had lots of brothers. Grace did, in fact,

have one less brother than Bacon.

6. Both men died before the First World War was over.

There will, of course, continue to be controversy about the claims that Mr. Pointer has made. We at the *Thomas Winsden's Cricketing Almanack* have decided not to change our statistical analysis of the career of W.G. Grace until more evidence is forthcoming.

# COLLECTOR'S CORNER

Books, scorecards, centenary plates, memorial tankards, cigarette cards, paintings, prints, photographs, stamps, bats, balls – the list of items sought and hoarded by collectors gets longer every year.

The latest hobby to attract cricket fanatics has been gum collecting (Masticmatics) and the London auction house, Sowerbys, has appointed a Curator of Chewing Gum to assess, value and authenticate items offered for sale. The publishers of *Thomas Winsden's Cricketing Almanack* asked the curator, Mr Arthur Wriggle, to prepare a list of some of the most interesting items in Sowerby's current collection.

Here is his choice.

### *1. The Trumpet Trophy (1911–12)*
A large, flattened gum relic taken from the back of Victor Trumpet's bat after the second innings of the Third Test in the England v Australia series of 1911–12. The gum was distributed with coupons entitling purchasers to buy plastic wicker hampers at reduced prices and was a special sugar-free variety manufactured by Dintone. Trumpet was a keen gum user who scored 1 not out while masticating this particular specimen. Records show that the gum was chewed for a total of 7 minutes before being attached to the back of Trumpet's bat.

## 2. The Bannaman Relic (1887–88)

A small, rather misshapen piece of gum enjoyed by the luckless Bannaman during the Sydney Test in which two English touring teams combined to play Australia. In their first innings Australia scored only 42 all out – Bannaman acquiring 2 of the runs while chewing this particular piece of gum. The gum was rescued from the dressing room at the Sydney ground in 1910 and it is believed to have been a relic of a stick shared with J.M. Blackman, the Australian wicket keeper. The whereabouts of the Blackman half of the relic is not known.

## 3. The Norse Keepsake (1921–22)

In the first Test between South Africa and Australia played at Durban in November 1921, Arbuthnot Norse scored 32 fine runs while giving a piece of early Wriggle Doublemint a tough time. After the match the gum was mounted on an ivory plinth and presented to Norse's mother. She later sold it to a Scandanavian tourist who, not realising the true value of the item, used it as a pin cushion for 17 years.

## 4. The Hendon Remainder (1929)

Beach Hut gum has always been popular with those cricketers who like their gum to have a little spine. The packet from which this piece of gum was taken was bought by Francis Woolly at the start of the third Test between England and South Africa in 1929. He bought it from Elsie Sidebotham who had a sweet shop outside the Headingley ground for 22 years.

The other pieces which were in the packet have long since been lost but this piece of gum, used by Hendon in the 2nd innings when he scored 5 runs has been passed from hand to hand in the Pilkington family since Elijah Pilkington picked the gum up from the spot where Hendon had thrown it in disgust as he made his way back to the pavilion.

### 5. The Hulton Souvenir (1947)

In the fourth Test of the series between England and South Africa in 1947, the great Norman Hulton scored 100 before being run out. Throughout that innings Hulton derived nourishment and pleasure from this enticing piece of Single Mint. At the end of the innings Hulton gave the gum to gateman Jonathan Forbes-Forbes, intending to retrieve it later. In the excitement, however, the gum was forgotten and it remained in the Forbes-Forbes family collection for over 35 years.

### 6. The Brandon Berg

The Great Don Brandon, the Spaniard who played his cricket for Australia, was a wildly enthusiastic gum chewer. In order to keep his concentration at its peak, he tended to use several pieces of gum at a time. Hence the popular name for this huge piece! Unfortunately, we have not yet been able to date the Brandon Berg, though carbon dating processes should soon make this possible.

### 7. The Washstand Residue (1947)

In the match between South Africa and England, played at Johannesburg in December 1947 (1947 was a good year for chewing gum) Cecil Washstand scored a majestic 195 in a partnership of 359 with Norman Hulton. He started his innings with a sliver of Wriggle no. 7, added a fresh slice of Don Tyne Mouth Moistener at lunch and completed the mouthful with a tantalising stick of Beach Hut at tea. After his innings Washstand was about to throw the accumulated gum away but fortunately was persuaded to hand it to a South African fan who preserved it in a cigar box for 30 years.

### 8. The Woolcott Stub (1950)

In the first West Indian innings of the 3rd Test at Trent Bridge in 1950 Freddie Warrell scored 261, Eddie Weeks accumulated 129 and the unhappy Alexander Woolcott managed only 8 runs. While scoring those 8 runs Woolcott tentatively nibbled at a piece of fresh Wriggle Triple Mint Gum. The gum still contains some of the original sugar coating and is considered to be a particularly fine collector's item. Most of Woolcott's stubs are very well chewed indeed.

## 9. The Beardsley Brick (1912)
Wilhelm Beardsley scored 164 in the first Australian innings of the 5th match in the Triangular Tournament of 1912. Playing against South Africa he ended up with an impressive five sticks of gum in his mouth. When he finally came back to the pavilion his jaw muscles ached so much that he needed oral physiotherapy.

# INJURIES ON AND OFF THE CRICKET FIELD

**By Professor H. Oaks F.R.C.S.**
*(The England Team's Official Neurocardiothoracophysiologist)*

The increasingly competitive nature of top class cricket has meant that in recent years a growing number of professional players have been leaving the field of play with injuries. During the last twelve months, for example, I myself have had to look after three hundred and seventy-six cricketers, suffering from a wide range of disorders. In an attempt to help my less-experienced medical colleagues, I have prepared a list of the ten most common problems.

## 1. Stretched nerves
The pressure on professional cricketers can be tremendous. With the number of spectators at first class county

matches sometimes reaching ten or even fifteen, it is hardly surprising that players suffer from stress. 'Stretched nerves' can be an almost chronic condition in players during the testimonial years. (See also *Testimonialitis*.)

## 2. Pushed hamstring
The pulled hamstring is, of course, very common. Professional cricketers often worry about their health (see *Hypochondriasis*) and often guard too energetically against this problem. The result can be an injury which is the mirror-image of the one the player was trying to avoid in the first place.

## 3. Testimonialitis
Professional players rely heavily on the money they expect to earn during their testimonial or benefit years. There are, however, considerable hazards to be faced. The player who has a testimonial year will often find that he has to attend dozens of dinners and dances. The testimonialitis syndrome can be easily identified by its principal symptoms which include a fixed grin, dull, lifeless eyes which seem to see nothing, spasms and twitches in the hand most commonly used for shaking and back-strain caused by carrying the money to the bank. (See also *Stretched nerves*.)

## 4. Congenital femurs
Surveys have shown that nearly all professional cricketers have femurs. The very existence of these bones means that they can be broken. This is a drawback professional cricketers have to learn to live with.

## 5. Herpes
Cricket groupies are very common in Hove, Manchester, Kennington and Cardiff. Herpes is a natural and inevitable risk.

## 6. Writer's cramp

Mainly affects cricketers when they're asked to sign autographs by small, scruffy boys clutching dirty pieces of paper and pencil stubs. The condition seems to go into remission when the cricketer is commissioned to write a newspaper article, sign a contract, dictate and sign his memoirs or endorse a bat, glove or cheque.

## 7. Recurrence of an old injury

If a professional cricketer leaves the field of play half-way through a match, then the chances are high that he will be suffering from 'a recurrence of an old injury'. The best treatment is to attempt to convince the player that in fact, he is enjoying the recurrence of an old recovery.

## 8. Haemodementia

Haemodementia affects cricketers who achieve more success than they can comfortably cope with. Bowlers suffering from haemodementia (or bloodymindedness as it is also known) will often grumble when they are invited to bowl but, on the other hand, complain bitterly if *not* invited to bowl. Haemodementia in batsmen can be diagnosed by a tendancy to find fault with their batting positions, their partners and their accommodation in the team hotel.

## 9. Plumbi Oscillans

A common condition that seems to affect cricketers only when they are fielding. It sometimes seems to be allied to a recurrence of an old injury.

## 10. Hypochondriasis

Very common among all cricketers. If they sneeze they feel convinced that they are about to contract pneumonia. If they suffer a mild backache, they are sure it signals the onset of sciatica. If they get indigestion, they *know* they are having a heart attack. If they have a nosebleed, then it's bound to be haemophilia. The only answer is to laugh at them and to refuse to listen to their pitiful drivelling.

Those listed above are the disabilities which most commonly afflict professional cricketers. Club and village cricketers display different signs and symptoms. I have prepared a list of the nine disorders which most commonly affect cricketers in the amateur category.

### 1. Pregnancy
This condition can have a devastating effect on the career of a female cricketer.

### 2. Twisted ankle
Usually affects fielders who are outfield specialists. Plough-furrows and rabbit holes are two common contributory causes.

### 3. Headache
A woman whose husband repeatedly comes home with grass stains all over his trousers will respond in one of two ways. She will either nag him for hours on end and provide him with a detailed description of the problems involved in removing grass stains from flannels (in which case he will end up with a headache), or she will cuff him round the ear (in which case he will end up a headache). Either way, grass stains cause headaches.

### 4. Indigestion
Anyone who washes down two dozen cheese sandwiches, three pickled eggs, two packets of crisps, a rock cake and a piece of fruit cake with sixteen pints of beer deserves indigestion. A good amateur captain will take care to monitor the food that his side intends to consume with its pints.

## 5. Food poisoning
Food poisoning can be avoided by steering well clear of meat paste sandwiches.

## 6. Dislocated shoulder
This painful and unpleasant condition usually develops when a forty-five-year-old medium-pace bowler, having been hit for six consecutive boundaries by a spotty sixteen-year-old batsman attempts to bowl a ninety mph bouncer at the batsman's grinning head. Captains of club teams should be aware of this hazard and intervene at the appropriate moment.

## 7. Broken finger nails
This irritating phenomenon is frequently suffered by fielders who cannot repress the reflexive response to a hard-driven ball and attempt to catch it, rather than turning away or shouting 'Yours' to a nearby team-mate. Women players tend to be particularly distressed by it and, for that reason, prefer to field in the slips or gully.

## 8. White, soggy skin
An unappealing cosmetic deficiency that affects players who spend too long in the bath.

## 9. Depression
Affects all club cricketers at the end of the season. If they have done well they will want the season to continue; if they have done badly they want the season to continue so that they can make an effort to prove that they are not past it after all. The depression is usually at its worst about one month after the season ends. It then lifts progressively, until the heady smell of newmown grass, the lilting call of the first cuckoo and the appearance of delicately-furred catkins among the budding hedgerows herald the arrival of spring and re-awaken

the cricketer's hibernating spirit and sense of joie de vivre. (Sorry, I got carried away).

# WHAT UMPIRES CARRY IN THEIR POCKETS

Have you ever wondered exactly what those fascinating bulges in umpires' pockets really are? Well, for the last twelve months the research staff here at *Thomas Winsden's Cricketing Almanack* have been carrying out a comprehensive, world-wide survey of the contents of umpires' pockets. Here are their results:

*1. The village cricket umpire's pockets contain:*
A handkerchief
A bit of fluff
A box of matches
A pipe
A tin of tobacco
A book of crosswords (in case the match gets boring)

*2. The club or league cricket umpire's pockets contain:*
A handkerchief
Seven small pebbles (six and a spare*)
Spare ball
Penknife (which contains attachment for getting horse-shoes out of boy scouts' ears)
Packet of sweets (mints or fruit gums)
Folding umbrella
Safety pin
Copy of the rules of cricket in a plain cover


*It is important to keep the seventh pebble in a separate pocket.

### 3. The first-class cricket umpire's pockets contain:

Two handkerchiefs

Six specially polished small pebbles or six small coins

Two spare balls (one suitable for use if the ball in play goes out of shape within the first sixty minutes of play and the other for use if the second ball goes out of shape too)

Spare bails

Light meter

Notebook and pencils for keeping track of overs bowled, warnings given, etc

Penknife (includes attachment for getting penknives out of club umpires' pockets)

Scissors

Sewing kit (includes cotton in three shades of white)

Small of bottle of aspirin tablets

Salt tablets

Sticking plaster (assorted sizes)

### 4. The Test cricket match umpire's pockets contain:

Three handkerchiefs

Six specially polished small pebbles brought back from Bondi Beach and/or six small Indian coins

Six spare cricket balls in various stages of wear

Spare bails

Spare set of stumps

Light meter

Spare light meter

Miniature tape recorder (for compiling material to go into memoirs, snatches of conversation, etc)

Spare tape recorder

Spare batteries for both recorders

Penknife

Spare penknife

Scissors (large, small, nail and pinking)

Sewing machine

Spare sewing machine

Sewing kit (includes cotton in 12 shades of white and 3 shades of grey)

Medicine kit (includes aspirin, paracetamol, kaolin, antihistamines, penicillin, cough linctus, calamine lotion, tetracycline, anti-dandruff remedy, bran, tranquilliser, stimulant, sedative, anti-malarial pills, rabies vaccine, oxygen cylinder)

Salt tablets

Pepper tablets

Sticking plasters (12 pink and 12 brown and 12 black)*

Suture kit

Pocket calculator

Comb

Hair brush

Torch

Spare batteries for torch

Shoe polish

Shoe repair kit

Spare shoe laces (18 inch and 24 inch, black and white)

Packet of trouser buttons

Packet of shirt buttons

Zip repair kit

Tape for mending cracked bats

Spare bats

Two way telephone (for consulting Prime Minister if decision seems likely to affect foreign policy or international relations)

Make-up bag

Moisturising cream

Grass seed

Sawdust (for damp patches)

Fertiliser (for bald patches)

Spare white coat (With all pockets filled. Contents of pockets include spare white coat)

*When playing in the Far East 12 yellow are also included.

# TEN UNFORGETTABLE SCORERS

## 1. S. Veniaminoff
Known as the 'Russian memory man', Veniaminoff was probably the only scorer to go through a whole season without writing anything down. At the drop of a bail he could give you any player's personal average. He scored in the Russian primary league for a total of eleven years.

## 2. A. Einstein
Although it isn't recorded in his official biography, Einstein was a keen cricket scorer. Unfortunately, while in his early forties, he managed to prove that the number of runs scored will always be $x = nk^2$ where x is the date, n the number of wickets falling and k the combined height of the fielding side. This formula ended Einstein's interest in cricket, for it meant that he always knew what the result was going to be before the match began.

## 3. Nigel Honeydew
This computer genius thought that he'd made a great breakthrough in scoring technology when he produced a pocket computer that seemed to make traditional methods obsolete. Unfortunately, the computer had to be discarded when it was discovered to be prone to error. Its most memorable mistake occurred during the 1978 series of Tests. In the Lord's match, England's second innings score was entirely deleted from the final total and could not be restored without reference to spectators' score cards.

## 4. Isaac Levy
Loved cricket and loved scoring but had an unusual habit of knocking 10% off every score.

### 5. G. Verdi
Hired in error by a team of Middle Europeans. His score was later performed at La Scala.

### 6. Man Friday
Employed by Robinson Crusoe as scorer in match against local team of savages. Unfortunately, Man Friday was illiterate and the score sheet was of little value.

### 7. Jeremy Ffolkes-Ffolkes
His superb copper plate handwriting made Jeremy Ffolkes-Ffolkes a marvellous scorer. Unhappily, he took so long to fill in the score sheet that in matches where he officiated it was rare for more than two overs to be bowled in a day.

### 8. Plum Whitestick
It is rare for a blind scorer to reach the top in this demanding profession but Whitestick did very well until deafness resulted in an early retirement.

### 9. Jimmy 'The Cricket Bag' Marello
Learnt his trade while working as No 2 in the New York numbers racket. Marello made a small fortune by changing score sheets and running a book on the side. Killed in a gang fight outside the pavilion at Lords during a one day final.

### 10. Ms Gretel Greet
Would have been a fine scorer if she'd been better at adding up. At the end of one match the home team had scored 987 for 13 in their first innings while the visitors had scored 16 for 472 wickets.

# TEN EXTREMELY FAMOUS AND IMPORTANT CAPTAINS

## 1. Captain Cook
First man to take a team to Australia.

## 2. Captain T.E. Lawrence
Led a very successful team known as The Arabs.

## 3. Captain Bligh
Had tremendous problems persuading his bowlers to bowl and could never persuade his batsmen to follow the official batting order. On one famous occasion, four batsmen opened the innings together.

## 4. Captain D.H. Lawrence
Sometimes confused with Captain T.E. Lawrence.

## 5. Captain America
Led a team which included Superman, Batman and Spiderman. Undefeated after 694 games.

## 6. Captain Nemo
Throughout his fourteen year career, never allowed a match to be disrupted by rain or bad light. Once played a match at Worcester when umpires sat in rowing boats.

## 7. Captain Singleton
Took teams to West Indies and India. Immortalised in a famous tour book written by cricket writer D. Defoe.

## 8. Captain Sensible
Never lost a match with a bad declaration. Cautious, methodical but unimaginative leader.

## 9. Captain Boycott
Unpopular Irish cricketer whose estate team never won a match.

### 10. Captain Scott
His polar team, attired in whites, were lost for 8 days during a blizzard. It was as a result of this disaster that cricketers started to wear coloured caps.

# THE TEN MOST INTERESTING SLOW BOWLERS OF ALL TIME

### 1. Niccolo Machiavelli
Gave the ball a tremendous twist. No-one ever knew what to expect. Would have taken more wickets if he had been prepared to appeal directly, but preferred to make oblique suggestions to the umpire via outfielders, spectators, etc.

### 2. Confucius
Would have played in more Tests if he hadn't developed a bad habit of stopping to deliver telling homilies to umpire, batsman, other fielders etc.

### 3. Tomas de Torquemada
Leg break specialist who played for a Spanish team. Broke 739 legs and got 739 confessions. An unequalled record.

### 4. Attila the Hun
Started life as a fast bowler but his height (he was a midget) made it difficult for him to get up much speed. Became a spinner in later career and used to approach the wicket on the back of an elephant. Nothing in the laws of cricket prevents this, but Attila was no-balled a great deal because he failed to train the elephant to keep an eye on the crease.

### 5. R. Bosanquet
The man who invented the googly later won additional fame as a news-reader. Found the secret of eternal youth. Some have suggested that he is, in fact, a descendant of the googly originator, but his ability to give a tremendous tweak to bread-rolls in restaurants scotches this errant theory.

### 6. T. Benn
Never actually completed a delivery. Would stand at the wicket and wave his pipe about while gibbering endless nonsense. Batsmen would leave the crease in an attempt to get away from his monologues. On three occasions entire teams retired 'too bored to continue'. Officially, an off-break bowler.

### 7. Rasputin
Bowled funny little chinamen which didn't fool players, but had a convincing way with umpires. By the end of a five day match batsmen would be given out before they'd left the pavilion.

### 8. George Bernard Shaw
Never bowled a ball in his life and shouldn't be in this list at all.

### 9. John Wayne
His unusual gait gave his action extra movement and ensured that batsmen never knew what to expect.

### 10. Nureyev
Few ballet dancers have played cricket with such panache. Nureyev used to stand at the crease and pirouette, then release the ball when he reached maximum speed. His problem was that he never showed much control and usually bowled in the direction of third man.

# THE EIGHT WORST FAST BOWLERS OF ALL TIME

### 1. Long John Silver
Managed to get up quite a speed but had a tendency to fall over three or four times in the course of an over. Had a habit of putting his leading crutch across the crease and was once no balled fifty-seven times in a single session.

### 2. M. Richebourg
Best known as a spy who made his mark during the French Revolution, Richebourg was also a demon fast bowler. His main problem was his height which limited his ability to get bounce out of the wicket. (He was only 1ft 11inches tall).

### 3. Captain Ahab
Bowled beamers and was banned for throwing at the heads of batsmen.

### 4. General Franco
Used to get very cross when his appeals were turned down. In the end no one would umpire in matches where he was bowling.

### 5. Quasimodo
Promising bowler who gave up the game after being called for throwing in the annual clerics v medics match at Longchamps.

### 6. Laloo
Indian player who had an extra set of arms and legs from a headless twin attached to his body at the neck. Got up a tremendous pace but often forgot which hand was holding the ball.

### 7. James Toller
English giant who was 8ft 6ins at his prime. Fast but erratic. Even when he bowled on a length, the ball would bounce so excessively that it invariably went for 6 byes.

### 8. W. Wordsworth
Could have been a fine fast bowler but got into the habit of taking a long run and stopping half way in to gaze at flowers in the outfield. Once took 4½ hours to complete a 6 ball over.

# TEN UMPIRES OF RENOWN

### 1. Pontius Pilate
Rather weak-willed. Inclined to vacillate and could be swayed by crowds and fielders.

### 2. Judge Jeffries
Quite the opposite to P. Pilate. Feared by players, spectators and fellow umpires. Left a trail of death and destruction behind him. After a particularly successful season, Jeffries retired leaving only four first class cricketers alive in England.

### 3. Horatio Nelson
Fine umpire but had a weak spot – just couldn't cope with left arm bowlers who went round the wicket. Was often completely unaware that they were bowling at all.

### 4. L. van Beethoven
Held up his index finger with tremendous flair but rarely heard appeals the first time and never heard a faint snick.

### 5. J. Milton

Not a good umpire. Could officiate in four languages at the age of six but his lack of vision was limiting.

### 6. Ayatollah Khomeni

Gave everyone out first ball. Never officiated in a match that lasted for more than sixteen minutes. Always insisted on giving the bowler the benefit of the doubt.

### 7. Idi Amin

Once batted, bowled and umpired in forty-six matches at once. Never gave himself out but always answered his own appeals in the affirmative. On three occasions also acted as a sight screen.

### 8. Sophocles

Never made a wrong decision.

### 9. Darth Vader

Starred in training film for umpires (The Umpire Strikes Back). Got into trouble with T.C.C.B. for refusing to wear a white coat.

### 10. Lady Macbeth

Umpired in mixed cricket. Gave the famous Jack Spot out lbw in the first timeless Test held in Australia.

# PRAYERS FOR CRICKETERS

For many years there have been strong links between cricket and the church. Now a group of clergymen have written a special prayer book which contains ninety-three prayers suitable for use by all cricketers. *Thomas Winsden's Cricketing Almanack* is proud to be able to include, in this year's edition, three of the prayers which will be most widely used.

## The Batsman's Prayer

Lord, please deliver me from all bouncers, bumpers and shortsighted umpires. Protect me in my adversity from poor light, damp patches on the wicket and excessively diligent fielding. Guard me against balls which bounce unexpectedly and against any loss of concentration. Give me the skill, the strength and the confidence to deal with balls which turn square, bowlers who glower in a threatening fashion and wicket keepers who talk incessantly. I pray, too, oh Lord, that you will see to it that at least one top class photographer will be on the ground should I be fortunate enough to score a century and I ask for the strength to help me cope with the enthusiastic fans who will, I pray, run out onto the pitch, pat me on the back and stuff paper currency into my trouser pockets whenever I reach a fresh milestone.

## The Fast Bowler's Prayer

Bless, oh Lord, my trusty ball;
Keep it red and shiny.
Bless my stride and keep it long,
And make my bowling tidy.

Bless my action, keep it sound;
Dull the batsman's senses.
In the wisdom, keep the ball
From reaching boundary fences.

Give me speed and give me bounce,
Let the batsman snick it.
Stop the umpire nodding off,
And help me take a wicket.

Thank you, Lord, for all your care,
And more for your attention.
When the batsman's on his way,
I know you'll get a mention.

**The Umpire's Prayer**
Lord, keep me awake to count
The balls in every over,
Let me be consistent, wise
And watchful as yourself, Jehovah.

Help me to stay alert for each
Snick or deviation.
Let me be consistent and
Untainted by temptation.

Lord, keep me vertical I pray,
And steady on my feet.
Let me be consistent, though
The batsman be a cheat.

Make me patient as a saint
When the day is boring.
Let me be consistent, though
Neither batsman's scoring.

These prayers are all taken from *The Cricketer's Prayer Book* (published by Synod Books). There are, in addition to these three prayers, special oblations for spin bowlers, groundsmen, fielders who have dropped catches, captains who keep losing the toss, batsmen who are consistantly run out and club secretaries trying to devise fixture lists.

# Cricket laws (revised)

### 1. The Team
There will be more or less eleven players to each side.

### 2. The Captain
One player will be captain and the others will be not. The captain is entitled to bat anywhere in the order, bowl when he feels like it and tell someone else to run after the ball if it passes near to him when he is fielding. By and large, the captain is never the fielder nearest the ball.

### 3. Substitution
Substitutes shall be permitted to field for any player who is incapacitated by illness, injury or commercial committment. Ageing, opening batsmen who have scored more than 2,000 runs in Test cricket and fast bowlers with more than 100 wickets in Tests may go off the field for up to ninety minutes at a time for a shower, change of clothing, discussion with publisher or ghost biographer, paid TV interview or a game of golf (not exceeding 9 holes).

### 4. Runner
A runner shall be allowed for a batsman who is incapacitated by illness, injury or fatigue. The player acting as a runner shall wear batting gloves, pads, elbow protectors, helmet with visor, chest protector, box, thigh pads, skin cream, shin pads, boots, socks, shirt, two sweaters,

jock strap, trousers, copper bangle to protect against rheumatism and a small gold chain with the batsman's initials on it.

### 5. Batsmen leaving the field
A batsman may leave the field at any time to dictate his account of memorable parts of an innings, to exchange bats if the manufacturer's trademark becomes obscured, or for any other cause deemed to be unavoidable by him and his agent. Batsmen claiming to be ill or injured may not leave the field unless unconscious or suffering from diarrhoea.

### 6. The umpires
Two umpires shall be appointed, one from each side, to control the game with matching partiality.

### 7. The wickets
Two sets of wickets, each consisting of three wooden stumps and each about this high and that wide, shall be pitched on fairly flat ground at a point roughly equidistant from all the boundary markers. The individual stumps should be placed in such a way that a normal sized ball won't quite pass between them. Wooden bails (about so big) should be balanced on top of each set of stumps.

### 8. Timing
The umpires shall agree to start the match at a convenient time and stop it when everyone has had enough. (See also *Cessation of Play*).

### 9. Position of umpires
The umpires shall stand on the field of play some distance from one another.

### 10. Fitness of ground, weather and light

In first-class cricket, the umpires shall be the sole judges of the fitness of the ground, weather and light. Play will not be allowed if there is a cloud in the sky, any moisture in the air or dew on the grass. There will be no cricket if the umpires cannot see a light meter at six hundred paces. If there are more than two thousand spectators in the ground then the light meter must be visible at eight hundred paces. (A pace is measured by the distance covered by a fast bowler in full flight, not by that covered by a batsman in returning to the pavilion). In local or club cricket the fitness of the ground, weather and light shall be determined by the majority vote of the players involved.

### 11. Signals from umpires

When an umpire wants to leave the field of play and relieve himself he will stand on one leg and look distinctly uncomfortable.

When an umpire wants to call for a tea interval he will impersonate a teapot by bending one arm upwards and touching the nearest shoulder with the tips of his fingers.

When an umpire wants to draw the scorer's attention to activity on the field of play he will wave both hands about at waist level.

When an umpire wants to attract the attention of a spectator, or sees someone he knows in the crowd, he will raise one hand above his head and wave it about.

### 12. Scorers

The scorers will watch the match most of the time.

### 13. The Ball

The ball shall be red, quite big and fairly heavy. In first class cricket matches a new ball shall be provided whenever the old one looks shabby, doesn't show up clearly on television or stops putting red marks on the bowlers clothes. In the event of a bowler becoming upset because he's taking few wickets, he may complain and have the ball changed. In village or club cricket a new ball shall be provided at least once a season.

## 14. The Bat
Batsmen shall be equipped with a bat or some other means to protect themselves whenever they have to face the bowling. Bats shall be made of wood and marked distinctively by the manufacturer.

## 15. The Pitch
The pitch is the area of the field of play where the grass is shortest and the ground is flattest. The groundsman shall paint white lines on the pitch so that the fielders know where to stand.

## 16. Rolling, Sweeping, Mowing and Watering the Pitch
The pitch shall be rolled, swept, mown and watered except during play.

## 17. Covering the pitch
The pitch shall not be covered during play.

## 18. Innings
Each side shall have one or two innings unless there is insufficient time in which case they will not. If one side can beat the other side without the need to bat twice then the batsmen in the first side shall bat only once.

## 19. The Toss
The captains shall toss for the choice of innings before the match starts. The winner of the toss shall tell the other captain what he has decided to do before the match starts and shall not change his mind very much.

## 20. Declarations
If any player makes an obscene or offensive declaration then he shall be reprimanded by his captain.

## 21. Start of play
Play will start when everyone is ready.

## 22. Intervals
Intervals for meals, cakes, buns and so on shall be taken whenever anyone is hungry or when it is raining.

## 23. Cessation of play
The day's play will end when everyone has had enough or earlier if there is anything particularly good on the television.

## 24. Scoring
A side who bats and bowls best will win. The scorers are responsible for arranging this.

## 25. Boundary
The boundary will be marked by bits of rope, scruffy little flags, hedges, fences, spectators, nearby buildings and fielders. In the absence of such markers then the field of play shall be deemed to finish at the point where the grass is more than six inches high.

## 26. Lost Ball
A ball is deemed lost if it cannot be found.

## 27. The result
When a ball has been deemed lost another must be found.

## 28. No ball
See lost ball.

### 29. Wide ball
The ball shall only be this big. If it is bigger than this then it is a wide ball and not allowed.

### 30. Bye
At the end of a match the players shall all shake hands and say 'bye'.

### 31. Appeals
A bowler shall only appeal if he thinks the batsman is scoring too many runs, is boring, could have been out earlier or should be out. He should appeal by screaming unintelligible gibberish, holding both arms high in the air and glaring first at the batsman and then at the umpire. The batsman is entitled to look as peeved as he likes and the umpire is the only person whose opinion is worth a dollop of boot blanco.

### 32. Caught
A batsman is said to be given out caught if the bowler and at least one more fielder can convince the umpire that a catch has been taken.

### 33. Leg Before Wicket
A batsman shall be given out leg before wicket if the ball, after pitching on the ground, hits, or appears to hit, any part of his person and the bowler's appeal is particularly convincing.

### 34. The Wicket Keeper
The wicket keeper shall be responsible for providing the stumps and making sure that they are kept varnished and free of dirt.

### 35. Unfair play
Anything that isn't cricket isn't cricket.

# Book reviews

**Next Year's Season by R. Fawke-Astor** *(Future Perfect Press £9.05)*
For years now, publishers have been struggling to hasten the appearance of books containing information about the previous season. Astrologer and cricket-writer R. Fawke-Astor has gone one better. This remarkable volume contains first class averages and results for *next* year's season – published and in the shops before the players have even begun to warm up, or flex their flabby muscles. In the press release which accompanies *Next Year's Season* the publishers announce that they intend to publish fresh volumes every season. They also promise to accompany next year's edition with a compendium of some of the most interesting match reports for the next ten years.

**The Forward Defensive Stroke by Sir G. Boikes** *(Laundry Press £6.01)*
An illustrated coaching manual in which England batsman Sir G. Boikes explains the history of the forward defensive stroke and shows how beginners can achieve a high level of proficiency with only ten hours of practice a day. (4 action photographs).

**Pavilion Design by Victor E. Arnour** *(Tinhutt Books at £8.01)*
A 'must' for the aspiring pavilion designer. Over the years, Mr. Arnour has both designed, and supervised

the building of, everything from flat-roofed tin sheds to vast edifices constructed for Asian princes.

The book is wonderfully well-illustrated, with detailed depictions of bricks, bags of cement and close-ups of RSJs. Essential information on putty mixing and lino laying is included, together with a comprehensive section on how to create Doric columns out of simple polystyrene.

A special section gives elaborate details of the two most important areas in any well-thought-out pavilion: the bar and the Chapel of Rest. A gem of a book!

### Linseed Oil Through the Ages by Dr. T.E. Braille
*(published by Thames House at £17.01)*
Linseed oil is something that most of us take for granted. And yet did you know that there are forty-three different types of linseed oil? Or that the best temperature for using linseed oil is three degrees below body heat? Were you aware that the person who first discovered that linseed oil has a useful effect on cricket bats was Captain Cook – the famous inventor of Australia? Those are just some of the facts in my nephew's enthralling book.

### Wines of the World (price includes 1 doz crates of assorted wines) by S & H Palate *(Vintner Presses £2,386.37)*
It might seem odd to include this book among those under review, but the fact is that too many cricketers are prone to make fools of themselves in high society, by ordering pints of Chateau la Tour or asking for Spanish Reisling.

I found it, and the accompanying samples, very instructive and can heartily recommend it to all who might at some time be mixing with rich sponsors. It's a full-bodied, light, dry little book without a hint of pretentiousness. I look forward to the new edition.

**Just a Lanarkshire Lad by F. Truman** *(Arthur Pelham Books £6.10)*
The frank, fearless story of a young man's rise to fame as he yanks himself up by his bootlaces and fights class-prejudice, racial intolerance and crushing poverty. When young Fred starts his career as a hostile opening batsman, he finds that he is expected to do all the running between the wickets while the man at the other end, an experienced, senior professional, chats to the umpire or the wicket keeper. Fred never forgets the hardships he endured as an apprentice and when he becomes a Test player himself he always has a kindly word of encouragement for new batsmen as they struggle up and down the pitch endlessly running themselves out. Natural and heart warming.

**Rollo's Year by Rollo Verbatoven** *(Rollo Verbatoven Books, no price given)*
A dreary account of one man's year. Rollo watches Percy Sledge clean his bats in March and watches him get them dirty in May. He sees the great man score 33 not out for Rutland seconds in July and is present at the retirement dinner when Sledge is given a copy of last year's annual report signed by the treasurer and is presented with a tear off calendar.

**Memories of Lords by M.R. Davis** *(Pawn Books £2.05)*
No punches are pulled in this hard-hitting story of sexual excesses, bondage and peer group sessions. Names and places are named and placed and positions are fully illustrated. The searching forward is written by Lord Pilsbury who also happens to be almost the only member of the Upper House to avoid mention.

**Grounds for Divorce by Brenda Mengele** *(Engima Books £6.05)*
Brenda Mengele has written a moving account of the

breakdown of her marriage. For fifteen years the Menge-
les enjoyed an open relationship, allowing one another a
remarkable amount of sexual freedom. Then Brenda
Mengele discovered that instead of spending three days
a week with his blonde, buxom and long legged Brazilian secretary Fifi, her husband was secretly playing cricket. Once she'd overcome the initial shock, Brenda hired a private detective and the remaining two thirds of
the book is taken up with a detailed account of the
grounds they visited together. There is a particularly
poignant vignette describing her husband sitting, padded
up, at Trent Bridge one July. In the book's final chapter
Mrs Mengele explains how the divorce papers were delivered at Grace Road, Leicestershire and the Decree
Nisi handed to her husband while he was watching the
third day of a Schweppes County Championship Match
at New Road, Worcester. Natural and heart warming.

### The Toss by Patricia Keene *(Picture Books Ltd, £19.09)*
Never before has there been so beautifully illustrated
an account of the history of the toss. In this short volume, experienced photographer, illustrator and cartoonist
Patricia Keene has managed to capture the essence of
over a hundred years of tossing. There is a facsimile of
the coin used by W.G. Grace as a schoolboy fitted into
a special wallet at the front of the book as an added
incentive to collectors.

Photographs of coins similar to those used by Jar-
dine, Bradman, Brearley and Chapell all give this book
a very special quality which historians will savour.

There are, in addition, chapters dealing with How to
Toss and Diseases associated with Tossing. The first of
these two chapters deals with thumb flick techniques
favoured over the decades, while the second includes
notes on such disorders as coin tosser's thumb and
copper-induced digit dermatitis.

## 101 Uses For Grass Cuttings by Herbert Loam
### (Garden Books £15.05)

Any groundsman will confirm that if there is one com-
modity he has in abundance it is grass cuttings. In this
well-illustrated pamphlet, Herbert Loam (for 23 years
head groundsman for the Isle of Skye Parks Depart-
ment) has described some of the ways in which those
grass cuttings can be used to good effect.

## Spread Thinly But Spread Well by Anna Rechsea
### (Potit Books £1.05)

Any girl whose boyfriend or husband is keen on cricket
should make sure that she reads this book from cover
to cover. It is packed with instructions on the gentle art
of sandwich making, including separate chapters dealing with cheese sandwiches, egg and cress sandwiches,
ham sandwiches, egg and tomato sandwiches, cheese
and tomato sandwiches, ham and tomato sandwiches,
cheese and cress sandwiches, egg and ham sandwiches,
egg, cress and tomato sandwiches and cheese and ham
sandwiches. There is a section offering advice about
the needs of the lone spectator and the author includes
advice on such problems as how to cope with religious
dietary laws, how to deal with the requirements of cricketers with food allergy problems and how to keep a
drum of mayonnaise fresh for the entire season. Finally, there is a rather controversial afterword posing the
pros and cons of white vs. brown bread and whether
sliced or unsliced loaves should be used. Ms Rechsea
herself, a widely experienced sandwich maker, admits
that although she prefers using brown, unsliced loaves
she often finds herself forced to use white sliced bread
in order to cope with heavy demands.

## Basic Statistics by Wilhemina Frindly (Biggbooks £9.01)

Did you know that one of Derbyshire's reserve wicket-keepers takes size thirteen shoes? Did you know that Alan Griddle of Yorkshire has a thirty-two waist and a twenty-eight inch chest? And did you know that one of Surrey's most successful medium pace bowlers has thighs which measure a staggering twenty-two inches each?

These are just some of the fascinating titbits of information available in this wonderful collection of basic cricket statistics. It really is a must for any girl who has ever wondered what goes on under those white shirts and flannels. Ms. Frindley is apparently busily putting together a selection of even more intimate statistics for next year's edition.

### The Backward Defensive Stroke by Lord Boikes (*Laundry Press £6.05*)
An illustrated coaching manual in which Lord Boikes explains the history of the backward defensive stroke and shows how beginners can achieve a high level of proficiency with only sixteen hours practice a day. (6 action photographs).

### Pommelled to Death by Sydney Hill (*Abbo Books and Records £14.01A*)
A former Australian Test star describes his painful experiences during the infamous and now largely forgotten bodyline series of 1924.

### The Season's Greatest Moments by Canon O. Peneux (*Spire Press £5.01*)
When two men dressed in a camel costume ran onto the pitch at Headingley during last summer's England v Pakistan match, Oliver Peneux was there. He was present at Edgbaston when a hundred and fifty drunken clergymen managed to turn over sixteen cars in the Members' Car Park.

Blessed with a knack of being in the right place at exactly the wrong time Canon Peneux has been able to record most of last season's dramatic moments from the point of view of the ordinary spectator. His story is modestly told and includes a description of the memorable day when two umpires, officiating in a Test Match at Lords, fought a pitched battle on the pavilion stairs and left a hundred and twenty-seven members dead and seriously injured. He also describes the occasion when policemen fought an eight hour battle with the Headingley Seven – gatemen at the Yorkshire ground who refused to allow the policemen into the ground without individual passes.

Natural and heart warming.

### The Ayes Have It by Mohr Wyckitts *(Influential Publishers £11.01)*

In a book that could revolutionise appealing throughout the world Mohr Wyckitts, the famed hypnotist, shows how umpires can be influenced in a number of ways. He extols the virtues of deep eye control and describes how a formerly unsuccessful medium pace bowler took 116 wickets (all given out lbw) after just three lessons in the use of primary hypnosis techniques.

### Swing – a review by Duke Ellington *(Jazz Books £3.05)*

Seems to have been sent to us by mistake.

### Running Between the Wickets by H.R.H. the Prince of Boikes *(Laundry Press £6.05)*

An illustrated coaching manual in which H.R.H. the Prince of Boikes explains the history of running between the wickets and shows how beginners can achieve a high level of proficiency with only eighteen hours practice each day. There are chapters entitled 'Calling', 'Changing your mind', 'Changing your mind yet again' and '101 ways to say sorry'. The forward is written by Ms Denise Comptoir. (Eight action photographs and two inaction photographs).

# Obituaries

## Samuel Blockettt (1887–1983)

For nearly sixty years Samuel Blockettt had one of the most important jobs in English cricket. It was Samuel's responsibility to walk around the pavilion at Lord's half an hour after the end of every match day and carefully shake each remaining member in an attempt to differentiate between the quick and the dead. He had a quiet, gentle way with him and would begin each investigation by tapping the member on the shoulder with the forefinger of his left hand. If that failed to produce any movement he would murmur a few words in the member's ear – usually choosing something like 'Good shot, sir' or 'Well played, sir', in the hope of stimulating a similar, if automatic, response. If his efforts continued to be unrewarded, Samuel would carefully 'help' the former member out of his seat and down into the morgue in the pavilion basement. (Lords, incidentally, is probably the only cricket pavilion in the world to have its own morgue and full time mortician. Although the existence of this morgue is kept secret it's thought that it is busier than most big city morgues.)

Samuel himself died as he would have wished. He always sat directly behind the sightscreen at Lord's, from which position he claimed to be able to keep an eye on those members most likely to need his attentions. When he was found by his assistant on the second day of the Test last summer, rigor mortis had set in.

A memorial service will be held in the Lords Pavilion.

## Brigadier L.F.T.Y. McPherson (1881–1983)

In his younger days Brigadier McPherson (he wasn't Brigadier then, of course) played cricket for the Old Boys of St. Michael's School, Bond Street. His impressive figures (2 for 93 in his first full match and 17 wickets at a cost of 117 runs apiece in his first full season) were a tribute to his accuracy and control. Although primarily a bowler, Brigadier McPherson was also an elegant and forcing batsman, who once scored a majestic 25 not out in a match played in his brother in law's garden. (His brother in law, incidentally, was the famous wicketkeeper and slow bowler Archie Grubb who always kept to his own bowling).

Although he suffered from terminal lassitude in later life, Brigadier McPherson played for a number of army sides and continued to take an active part in the game for as long as he could. In his last year as a player the Brigadier would arrange for someone else to run up to the wicket for him so that he could bowl medium pace from a standing start.

Brigadier McPherson died on the first day of the Lord's Test last summer but owing to the demise of Samuel Blockettt his death was not discovered until the end of the fifth and final day of the match.

A memorial service will be held in the Lords Pavilion.

## Col P.W.K.L.S.R. Langtree (1883–1983)

Few men have given as much to the game of cricket as Colonel 'Piggy' Langtree. After falling in love with the game when an older boy at school taught him how to hold a ball properly behind the school bicycle sheds, Langtree spent up twenty minutes a day practising.

By the time he was twenty-seven, he had won a regular place as a reserve in the local colts team and in 1919 he played his first full match for his Regiment. He scored several runs on a number of occasions and often got close to taking a wicket. In his later years when he could no longer play the game he still loved so much, Langtree tried to give back to cricket some of the delight it had offered him. For nearly 40 years he sat on the Works and Car Park Sub Committee of the South Humberside Wanderers XI, on the Rules and Disciplinary Committee of the South East Budleigh Salterton Cricket Club and on the Special Sub-Committee of the Notting Hill Committee for Racial Equality in Sports Administration.

A memorial service will be held in the Pavilion at Lords.

### Mr Jim Bigdale (1922–1983)

Bigdale played for England 73 times and took 249 wickets at an average of 7.333. He scored 8,954 runs for his country at an average of 137.83.

There will be no memorial service.

### Rev. P.R.A. Young (1881–1982)

The death of one of cricket's foremost poets has left a tremendous gap in the world of cricket literature. Few modern writers have done so much to improve the standard of cricket reportage as Phil Young and no modern anthology would be considered complete without a line or two from 'the little master' as he was affectionately known by his colleagues.

Born into a cricket loving family, Phil Young learned his cricket at Wichampton School and played for the school second XI until he left for Cambridge. At university he spent his summers writing about cricket, rather than playing, and his articles on the subject often found their way into the magazine he edited.

After university Young went first to theology college and then to work for the up-and-coming *Bradford Guardian* which was an exclusively local paper at the time. Writing obituaries, advertising features and gossip column snippets left Young little time for his first love, but in the summer season, when the courts were in recess, he somehow managed to pen a line or two. Those were his salad days and much of what he wrote then was collected into the privately printed 'Green be my cricket field'.

One of his most famous poems *The match is won* was written during the Lords Test of 1912. A few lines of that poem are worth reproducing here:
The batsman swings, the children cry,
To see such perfect action.
The fielder swoops and makes a stop
And that's another match won.

Those lines won Young the adoration and respect of all his colleagues on the boundary-edge. For the next few years the young poet contributed to most of the major reviews of the day but still he considered his allegiance to be principally to the *Bradford Guardian* which had given him his first chance. It was there that the famous editor David 'Blue Pencil' Harsent worked with him and helped him develop his unique style of writing.

In the early 1930s Phil Young wrote another poem, *Watchers weak inside*. The poem was very controversial; in fact some critics claimed that it contained evidence of Young's latent homosexuality. The lines they pointed to in particular, read:
Tall, blond, strong and handsome,
The batsman stood with pride.
His rich and lordly bearing
Made watchers weak inside.

Now Phil Young is no longer with us. It is difficult to believe that we have lost a writer of such stature. He had spent the last three months of his life on a poem that was to have been his major work. The poem was unfinished but we are proud to print here the lines which Young had completed:

Oh, for the eyes of a batsman
Oh, for the arms of a bowler
Oh for the legs of a fielder.
. . . .

We can only speculate about the greatness that might have been had Young been granted time to complete this work.

### Roderick St. Spurry (1959–1982)
At the age of eighteen, Roderick St. Spurry celebrated his birthday by turning up for a club cricket match dressed as the rear half of a pantomime horse. When it was his turn to bat he trotted out to the wicket leaving behind him a trail of fluffy brown cotton wool balls. Between that spectacular beginning, and his early death last year, Roderick St. Spurry never tired of playing practical jokes on those around him.

At a crucial moment in one match, for example, he substituted a pomegranate for the cricket ball. The batsman at the receiving end thought it was so funny that he nearly had a heart attack and had to retire. On another occasion, Roderick used a ball which had one side glazed with high gloss red paint and the other roughened with sandpaper. The umpire thought that was a tremendous jape; so, once the joke had been explained to them, did the six batsman who had been dismissed with the ball.

One of Roderick's favourite jokes was to quietly tie a batsman to his wicket while the bowler ran up. That always went down very well. Another trick was to mix up all the shoes and boots in the changing room.

Roderick St. Spurry died last summer at the remarkably early age of twenty-three. According to the signed statements of twenty-one other players and two umpires. Roderick accidentally impaled himself on a set of stumps after bumping his head several times against his bat.

There will be a memorial service every April Fools Day.

## Harold Twigmorton (1902-1982)

His cricketing talents may have been limited, and the opportunities to display such skills as he possessed may have been few, but there can rarely have been a cricketer with a greater love for the game than Harold Twigmorton.

It is difficult to know just how to describe Harold's affection for cricket. Suffice it to say that although he was married for sixty-three years, Harold never took his protective box off during the cricket season (except on Saturday nights when he would dunk the contents of the box in a zinc hip bath half filled with lukewarm, soapy water). Harold argued that he always wanted to be ready in case he was called to play in an impromptu game. 'I may not be the best,' he was wont to say with commendable modesty, 'But they know they can rely on me if they're short of a man.'

So keen was Harold to be prepared, that for two months prior to the start of each cricket season the Twigmorton's bed would be graced by the presence of Harold's ageing but much loved willow blade. Harold would keep a thermos flask filled with warmed linseed oil in his bedside cabinet and each night the bat would be oiled with a loving caress that Mrs Twigmorton secretly envied.

When Harold and his bat were cremated the remains were spread on a good length on the local village pitch.

## Errata

There were several errors in last years edition of *Thomas Winsden's Cricketing Almanack*. The most significant were as follows:

Kent not Sussex won the Banker's Trophy.

Nottinghamshire not Warwickshire won the Sailor's League.

Surrey not Middlesex won the You-Know-Who County Championship.

Derbyshire not Yorkshire won the Gold Pack Cup.

England won the Test series and not Australia.

Willis was not top of the country's batting averages.

Yorkshire did not field seven Australian Test players.

Tasmania did not win the Currie Cup.

Pages 4 to 116 were numbered in reverse order by mistake.

The photograph of Clive Lloyd was actually a photograph of Barry Richards.

The photograph of Doug Walters was actually a photograph of the Pakistani touring team to New Zealand.

The photograph of Geoff Boycott actually was a photograph of Geoff Boycott, but it was the wrong Geoff Boycott.


A full list of errors and corrections will be sent to readers on receipt of a £2 postal order to cover the cost of postage and packing. Alternatively please send a piece of addressed wrapping paper with stamps affixed to cover a parcel weighing 700 g.

*YOU'VE TESTED*
*THE WINSDEN BATTING MACHINE*

*NOW!*

## WINSDEN UMPIRING MACHINE

* HOLDS SIX LONG-SLEEVED AND TWELVE
SLEEVELESS SWEATERS
* RUNS BACKWARDS (MAX. SPEED 40 MPH)
* STARES REPROACHFULLY
* GIVES HAND SIGNALS, INCLUDING LEG BYES
* VANDAL PROOF
* COMES COMPLETE WITH INBUILT LIGHT-METER

# *Looking for trophies for your cricket club?*

Then why not choose an item from the PRACTICAL range of cups?

Made from durable 100% hard wearing plastic compound that is specially satinised in our Kenilworth factory — these cups will give years of service.

*UNIQUE DESIGN!*

*ACTUAL SIZE!*

### *FREE*

As a special introductory offer we are giving a matching saucer away with every cup purchased before the end of this offer.

You can't fail to SCORE with

# *Arrowsmith's*

*notebook and pencil set*

Everyone you meet will be impressed when you take out your slimline super-pencil with rechargeable end.
And you'll attract attention wherever you go when you produce your ruled notebook in special village green.

*Arrowsmith's notebook and pencil set.*
*Available from all good stockists.*

*You've seen the aluminium bat –*
*NOW TRY THE TITANIUM BALL.*

*Longer lasting*
*More penetrative*
*Available in six different colours*
*A major breakthrough for bowlers*

*From*
*Lilyballs Incorporated, Perth, Australia*

**FROZEN GROUND?**

**BLUNT STUMPS?**

Then you need the BRAD DONMANE automatic stump sharpener

From all good ironmongers

'It's a must for all groundsmen,' says John McEnroe. 'I'd never be without it again.'

# Thinking of STREAKING?

– then you need Winsden's "SKIN-TEX" Body Stocking for maximum effect with the minimum of legal problems.

(Pink only)

# THE REVOLUTIONARY ZXL 7000

## A breakthrough in scoring technology

'I heartily recommend the ZXL 7000 computer, says
Wilhemina Frindley, the famous scorer. 'It's made my
life a lot easier.'

The ZXL 7000 can deal with all your scoring problems
simply and without fuss.
Write to 4 Brook St, London W1 for full details.

The ZXL range starts at £800,000 (excl. VAT) with the

I've read for years. I am very much looking forward to the sequel.
Mrs G. Sunderland

ISBN 0 9503527 5 6    230 pages    £12.99

## BILBURY GRANGE
Vernon Coleman

The sequel to The Bilbury Chronicles. All the books in the Bilbury series can be read and enjoyed independently.

ISBN 0 9503527 7 2    247 pages    £12.99

## THE VILLAGE CRICKET TOUR
Vernon Coleman

A novel describing the adventures and mishaps of a team of cricketers who spend two weeks of their summer holidays on a cricket tour of the West Country, and who make up in enthusiasm for what they may lack in skill.

'If anyone ever manages to bottle the essence of village cricket he will very quickly scale the dizzy heights of personal fortune. In the meantime we read and write about it in the pursuit of understanding. Seminal reading here includes de Selincourt and Blunden and should now embrace Vernon Coleman's latest offering, a whimsical piece about the peregrinations of a village team on its summer tour ... all the characters are here, woven together by a raft of anecdotes and reminiscences and a travelogue of some of the most picturesque spots in the south west.'
The Cricketer

'Describes in hilarious fashion the triumphs and disasters of a Midlands team's tour of the West Country and there is not a little of Jerome K.Jerome in Mr Coleman's style.'
Worcester Evening News

'I enjoyed it immensely. He has succeeded in writing a book that will entertain, a book that will amuse and warm the cockles of tired hearts. And what a change it makes from the wearisome

cluckings of the current crop of cricket books with their grinding pomposity and, in many cases, their staggering lack of craftsmanship and originality.'
Punch

'A delightful book which also highlights some of the most spectacular scenery in Cornwall and Devon.'
The Cornishman

'Vernon Coleman is obviously a man who has enjoyed his cricket and over the years has committed to memory the many characters he has seen playing the game. He weaves them into the story as he charts the progress of his team's tour of Devon and Cornwall. The tale captures club cricket as everyone imagines it should be.'
Falmouth Packet

'Coleman is a very funny writer. It would be a pity if cricketers were the only people to read this book.'
This England

ISBN 0 9503527 3 X    173 pages    £9.95

## ALICE'S DIARY
### The Memoirs of a Cat

Alice is a mixed tabby cat whose first book sparkles with wit and fun and a rare enthusiasm for life. Whether she is describing her relationship with the human beings with whom she shares her life (there are two of them – described as the Upright in Trousers and the Upright who wears a Skirt), her relationships with her many cat friends or her (not always successful) attempts at hunting, no cat lover will fail to find her story enchanting. Most important, every reader will, for the first time, have an insight into what it is really like to be a cat.

Extracts from some of the hundreds of letters received:

'I have just finished reading 'Alice's Diary' and what a delight it was. We have three cats and I can say with all honesty that I could have been reading about them.'
Mrs W. Cheshire

'I have just received my copy of 'Alice's Diary' and really did enjoy every page. I have recommended it to several of my friends.'
Mrs C. London

'Each night I read one month of your diary to my husband and all three of our cats came to listen as well!'
Mrs G. Berkshire

'Please send copies of 'Alice's Diary' to the eleven friends on the accompanying list. It is a wonderful book that will give them all great pleasure.'
Mr R. Lancashire

'A delightful book. I thoroughly enjoyed it.'
Mr W. Midlands

'"Alice's Diary" is one of the nicest books I have read. She has wonderful insight. When do we get the next instalment? I can hardly wait. It really is an enchanting book.'
Mrs J. London

ISBN 0 9503527 1 3    142 pages    £8.99

## ALICE'S ADVENTURES
### The Further Memoirs of a Cat

After the publication of her first book Alice was inundated with fan mail urging her to put pen to paper once more. The result is this, her second volume of memoirs.

No one could have predicted what was to happen to Alice during this, the most eventful year of her life. Another must for cat lovers everywhere.

'I didn't think Alice could surpass her first book – but she has. I really loved 'Alice's Adventures'. The saddest moment came when I finished it. When will the next volume be ready?'
Mrs K. Somerset

'We have had cats for 30 years and Alice describes incidents which are so real that we nearly died laughing at them.'
Mrs O. Leeds

'"Alice's Adventures" is he loveliest book I have ever read. It captures everything brilliantly. Thinking back over the book I can't help smiling. I have never enjoyed a book as much.'
Mrs H. Edinburgh

'What a wonderful book. It was a real pleasure to read.'
Mr E. Exeter

Alice's Adventures – The Further Memoirs of a Cat
ISBN  0  9503527  6  4   133 pages   £8.99

## MRS CALDICOT'S CABBAGE WAR
### Vernon Coleman

Thelma Caldicot was married to her husband for thirty dull and boring years. Then, completely out of the blue, two police officers arrived at Thelma's house to break some sad news. That afternoon, while her husband was at a cricket match, she had become a widow.

Her ambitious son Derek soon appears on the scene, determined to interfere in every aspect of her mother's life. After thirty years of being dominated by her husband, it looks as though Thelma's son is about to step into his shoes and continue the good work.

But then something happens to Thelma Caldicot. After years of being pushed around and told what to do, she takes charge of her life and fights back.

Mrs Caldicot's Cabbage War is the poignant, warm and often funny story of an ordinary woman who finally decides to stand up for herself.

'... a splendid, relaxing read ...'
Sunday Independent

ISBN  0  9503527  8  0   150 pages   £9.95

# THE MAN WHO INHERITED A GOLF COURSE
## Vernon Coleman

Trevor Dukinfield, the hero of this delightful novel, is a young and not very successful journalist. Completely out of the blue, Trevor receives a letter informing him that he has inherited a golf course from an uncle he never knew he had.

You might think that this would have been welcomed by Trevor as extraordinarily good news. But then Trevor discovers the two slight snags which accompany his good fortune.

First, in order to keep the golf club under the rules of his uncle's will, Trevor has to play a round of golf in less than 100 strokes. Second, he has to find a partner to help him win a match play competition against two bankers.

Not particularly stringent conditions you might think – except that Trevor has never played a round of golf in his life, unless you count an hour spent on a crazy golf course in Weston-super-Mare.

"Another witty volume from the doctor who has successfully turned from medical topics to novel writing. The ... mix of anecdotes and moments of sheer farce make for an absorbing read"
Lancashire Evening Telegraph

"... another delightful and amusing story. I rate this one as the best of his twelve novels so far. His fans will lap it up."
Sunday Independent

ISBN 0 9503527 9 9          237 pages          £12.95.